The Art of Taming the Business

The Art of Taming the Business

Business Essays

Vallabhi EY

iUniverse, Inc.
New York   Bloomington

The Art of Taming the Business
Business Essays

iUniverse books may be ordered through booksellers or by contacting:

iUniverse
1663 Liberty Drive
Bloomington, IN 47403
www.iuniverse.com
1-800-Authors (1-800-288-4677)

Because of the dynamic nature of the Internet, any Web addresses or links contained in this book may have changed since publication and may no longer be valid. The views expressed in this work are solely those of the author and do not necessarily reflect the views of the publisher, and the publisher hereby disclaims any responsibility for them.

ISBN: 978-1-4401-1101-3 (pbk)
ISBN: 978-1-4401-1100-6 (ebk)

Printed in the United States of America

iUniverse rev. date: 4/13/2009

PREFACE

All the business chapters in this book were written as assignments by the author as an MBA (Management of Business Administration) student in University of Northampton. There are twelve altogether, some are essays and some are reports. Most of these were written with an intention that these could be published one day. Also the chapters were written with an idea that it should not just reach business readers but also general readers who want to know business or just have an interesting read.

The various chapters and the section of Business Management are given below:

- Chapters 1, 2 and 3 related to Operations Research
- Chapters 4 and 5   related to Marketing
- Chapter 6   related to Organizational Strategy
- Chapter 7   related to Managing Change
- Chapter 8   related to Cross Cultural Management
- Chapters 9 and 10 related to People Management
- Chapter 11   related to Corporate Finance
- Chapter 12   related to Leadership

The author believes that different departments in an organization cannot be detached or distinguished without overlaps from other departments. These subjects mentioned above are related to the important characteristics of the concerned subject and would be useful for any department of business as a whole.

The conclusion of the last chapter ends with words of Jesus Christ adapted to the business environment.

About the Author

The Author Vallabhi EY is a student of MBA in University of Northampton, UK. She was a computer software engineer who has worked in various Indian software companies and then chose to pursue higher studies. She did Master of Business Administration (MBA) in University of Northampton and is supposed to graduate in June 2009. Though the author writes fiction, non-fiction and poetry, this is her first book to be published.

Acknowledgements

I would like to acknowledge all the teachers of University of Northampton who taught me that business is all about supply and demand and that business is not just about jargons but is common sense, and that if one could get rid of their laziness it is quite evident.

Also, my parents who have seen me grow with caution and pride.

It is one of my attempts to share my learning to others with its own correctness and mistakes.

Dedicated to India & UK and the person I love the most!

OPERATIONS RESEARCH
(IN A SUPPLY CHAIN CONTEXT)

CHAPTER – I

PERFORMANCE MEASUREMENT IN CHRYSLER

1. INTRODUCTION

You never know from where you get motivating ideas, sometimes even children's basic lessons teach a lot of philosophy. One such is shown below from Lewis Carroll's "Alice in Wonderland":

Alice says to the Cheshire cat, "Would you tell me, please, which way I ought to go from here? Is this the right way?"

"That depends a lot on where you want to go," said the cat.

"I don't know where I'm going," said Alice...

"Then it doesn't matter which way you go," said the Cat.

"--so long as I get SOMEWHERE," Alice added as an explanation.

"Oh, you're sure to do that," said the Cat, "if you only walk long enough."

We many times in business lose focus and don't know where to go. To avoid this, experts emphasise on performance measurement and eventually manage it effectively. The term performance measurement is defined in various ways. However most of the definitions indicate that we need to measure the performance in order to improve the future position, processes and decisions. The chosen company is Chrysler, because of its history which spans for about 80 years and suggests a chequered picture. On the face of it, the company has shown a lot of technical innovations ahead of times and because of that even failed among the public. In a way it seems that the problem with Chrysler is that they some times did not strike a balance between Business Management and Engineering Innovations.

2. HISTORY OF CHRYSLER

The Chrysler Corporation, established in 1925 by Chrysler P. Walter, was the last of the "Big Three", others being the Ford Motor company which stood first and General Motors which stood second. The company survived for much of its history on the strength of its automotive engineering, Chrysler can claim hundreds of significant "engineering firsts" in automobile design over the company's lifetime, as many as General Motors and Ford combined. In 1934 Chrysler engineer Carl Breer created the Airflow inspired by watching the manoeuvres of aeroplanes at an air show. During the 1950s Chrysler continued to come up with various auto engineering innovations. Chrysler's superiority over other car manufacturers can be proved by the fact the Chrysler C-300 was banned from sanctioned racing due to its massively superior engine power. During 1980-90, Lee Iacocca became the face of Chrysler to drive the core values of the company which includes affordable reliability. During the 1990-2000, Daimler-Benz bought Chrysler and the partnership proved to be successful (Bluesky Interactive, 2008).

3. DIFFERENT PERFORMANCE MANAGEMENT SYSTEMS

The managers of the late 1980s and early 1990s became extremely receptive to the fact that the performance measurement systems they have been using have in fact become obsolete. Statistics say that there were about 3,615 papers on performance measurement between 1994 and 1996 that were published which is equal to one paper published for every 5 hours of every working day (Neely, 1999). So, this period is considered to be the period of Performance Measurement Revolution period. Around 40 to 60 of organizations transformed to new performance measurement systems during 1995 and 2000 (Lardenoije *et al*, 2005). The important performance measurement systems are the Balanced Score Card, Performance Prism and Performance Pyramid. We will study these elaborately.

a) *Balanced Score Card (BSC*

Before the 1990s, only the financial figures were used to measure performance. And in due course, the importance of non-financial elements were used and a balance was measured using Balanced Score Card. BSC is one of the widely used performance measurement system which was developed by Kaplan and Norton. This system includes Key Performance Indicators in both financial and non financial areas. There are four building blocks that comprise the BSC and they are measured in terms of Objectives, Measures, Targets and Initiatives and their relationship are shown below (Lardenoije *et al,* 2005):

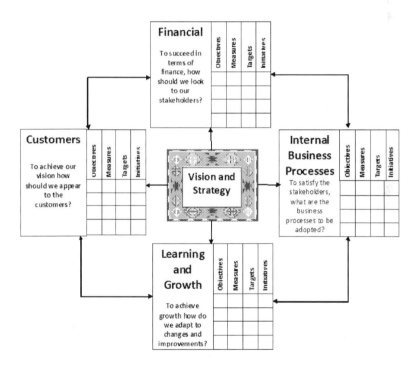

Figure 1.1: Balanced Score Card

Kaplan and Norton developed the Balanced Score Card and to

start with a little attention to process and eventually giving more importance to process (Neely *et al*, 2000).

b) *Performance Prism (PPR)*

The performance prism (PPR) was developed by Neely and Adams (2000) is a PMS organized around five distinct but linked perspectives of performance: stakeholder satisfaction, strategies, processes, capabilities, and stakeholder contributions. These are represented in a three dimensional Prism where the stakeholder's satisfaction and contribution forms the triangles in the prism and the other three form the three sides linked with the triangles. In practice, the performance measures are not unidirectional, so the three dimensional representation of performance prism indicates the complexity (Lardenoije *et al*, 2005).

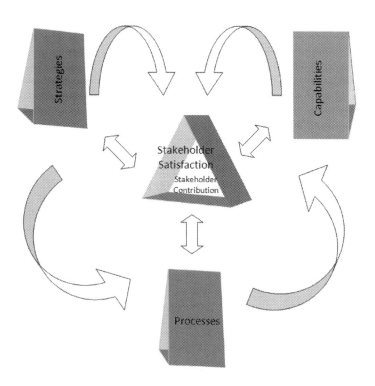

Figure 1.2: Performance Prism (Neely and Adams, 2002)

c) *Performance Pyramid System (PPS)*

The Performance Pyramid System is one of the foremost PMS developed by Lynch and Cross in 1991 during the Performance Measurement Revolution. This system explains the different variables at different levels of the organization. While strategic objectives flow downwards, the information flows upwards. Each level has its own objectives and measures. The four levels are corporate vision, accountability of the business units, competitive dimensions for business operating systems, and specific operational criteria which is represented in the form of a pyramid below (Lardenoije *et al,* 2005).

Figure 1.3: Performance Pyramid System (Neely *et al,* 2000)

d) *Comparison Report:*

The differences of the above mentioned Performance Measurement Systems are shown below (Lardenoije *et al,* 2005):

	Balanced Score Card	Performance Prism	Performance Pyramid
Advantages	The BSC explicitly focuses on processes.	The stakeholders other than customers and share holders are recognised to exist.	In the four levels, it includes Strategic Level to the Operational level.
Disadvantages	Lacks financial data like Risk Assessment and Cost-Benefit information.	The operational level details are not explained well.	This system has not been empirically tested (Metawie and Gilman, 2005)
	All three lack individual level feedback and motivation.		

4. PERFORMANCE MEASUREMENT IN CHRYSLER

The balanced scorecard, while initially developed to improve performance measurement, is now being used as a powerful tool for rapid and effective strategy implementation. The main gap in organizations is the lack of coordination in management structures. Organizations like Chrysler came up with a business unit called Office of strategy Management (OSM). The OSM is supposed to coordinate the following nine strategy execution processes which are explained in detail below (Kaplan and Norton, 2005):

a. *Score Card:*

The OSM is the owner of the Balanced Score Card of the organization with several responsibilities. The updated strategy communicated after the annual general meeting is translated to objectives, measures, targets and initiatives. Also, the OSM promotes learning and development about the BSC methodology and tools all through the year. The process of data collection and reporting across various departments are also managed by OSM. The standardisation of balanced score card terminology, measurement definitions, metric owners, who collects the data and report it on what frequencies, coordinate with internal audit department, so that the score card built on information is valid, reliable and auditable (Kaplan and Norton, 2005).

b. *Organization Alignment:*

This responsibility includes cascading the various strategies across different hierarchical levels. The synergies that needs to be created from the lower levels of the organizations are included in the corporate score card. Also, the individual business unit strategies and score cards and the support unit strategies have to be linked to the corporate strategy. The external stake holders like the customers, suppliers, joint ventures, board of directors have to be linked to the strategy of the organization (Kaplan and Norton, 2005).

c. ***Strategy Communication:***
The strategy, the map of strategy, the measures, targets, initiatives have to be communicated to employees through messages. The training about BSC has to be included in the training programs for employees. The messages for the employee have to be written and reviewed by the OSM and should be sent from the CEO or the local unit head so that the communication is effective (Kaplan and Norton, 2005).

d. ***Strategy Reviews:***
Instead of overemphasising the short–term financial performance, the OSM in case of meetings brief the CEO about the strategic issues identified in the most recent BSC, set the agenda for the meeting, find out the action plan, and follow up the meeting to make sure the actions are implemented (Kaplan and Norton, 2005).

e. ***Initiative Management:***
Initiatives have to be cross-functional and inter organizational, and should help to achieve strategic objectives. These strategic initiatives have to be managed to improve the BSC measures and should report the progress made. The initiatives should make sure they have enough resources, priority, and focus especially initiatives that are cross functional and cross departmental (Kaplan and Norton, 2005).

The above mentioned five processes are typically new for companies and are the responsibilities of OSM. But there are other processes which should be part of the organization which are usually under the department or unit. For these processes the OSM acts as co-ordinating agent and not a primary mode.

f. ***Strategy Development and Update:***

The strategies have to be reviewed periodically during meetings. The cause-and-effect hypotheses of the strategies between the internal actions and the expected impact on external constituents like customer and shareholders should be validated. After validation, the strategies have to be updated. Also, the emerging strategies within the organization have to be received and filtered and the strategy map and score card should be updated (Kaplan and Norton, 2005).

The integration of strategy development and execution responsibilities have been looked into, but the OSM has three more responsibilities to connect the planning, the budgeting, compensation component and knowledge sharing to contribute to the strategy.

g. ***Planning and Budgeting:***

The functional plans of HR, IT investments and Marketing programs are usually narrow and tactical, which are only operational and not strategic to the organization. So, an external body like OSM can align the functional strategy to the corporate strategy.

h. ***Employee Alignment:***

The employee's goals and ambitions have to be linked to the strategy of the organization. This also enhances the human capital of the organization. The employee focussed processes like communication, goals, compensation pack, and personal and leadership development have to be aligned and make strategy part of everyone's job.

i. ***Knowledge Management:***

The OSM should help to identify and transfer the best practices throughout the organization, helping to put across ideas in various departments, functions and business units (Kaplan and Norton, 2005).

The graphical representation of the relationships of the various dimensions of Balance Score Card and the different responsibilities of OSM are shown below:

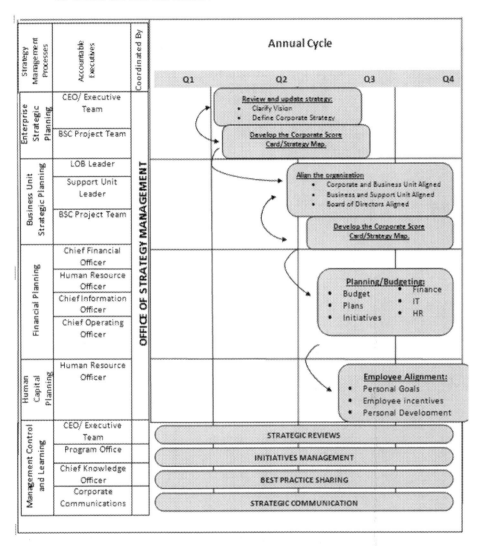

Figure 1.4: The components and responsibilities of OSM

5. ANALYSIS OF THE PMS IN AUTOMOBILE INDUSTRY:

For obvious reasons, the major problem with the Performance Measurement system in Chrysler that it did not take into account the supplier as prominent stake holder which in fact showed its adverse effect in Feb. 2008, when the Windsor assembly plant of Chrysler had to be shut down because of the strike in the Canadian Auto Workers which provides key components to Chrysler. This let some 4,400 workers of Chrysler idle (Morath, 2008). The inclusion of all stake holders including suppliers is addressed in the performance prism. But the individual feedback and motivation to some extent are addressed in the OSM concept.

If you take the example of Indian auto sector, the performance measures can be represented as below:

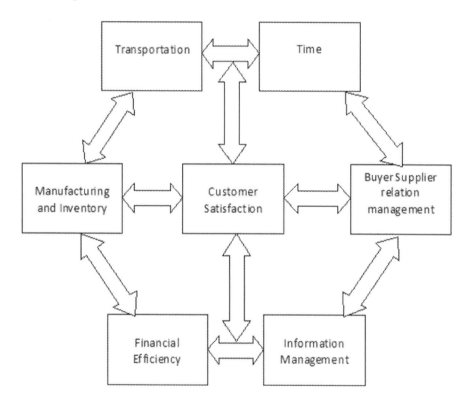

Figure 1.5: Performance measurement components of Indian Auto Sector

From comparing the case of Chrysler and an Indian manufacturer, the

Indian organizations have still not taken into account the employee as a prominent stake holder in the operations. Also, the transportation and information management are significant costs in the Indian context. In the past few years, auto assemblers have invested in their supplier base to enhance performance through developing lasting and stable relationships. (Patel and Saad, 2006).

When comparing the buyer-supplier relationships in American automotive industry and Japanese automotive industry it has been found that the GM attempted to save costs by encouraging competition among suppliers, which saved cost in short term had adverse effects in long term. In the other hand, the Japanese manufacturers like Toyota and Nissan followed the partnership model. Toyota, for instance, guarantees future business for the suppliers and hence developed a long term relationship. In turn the suppliers made some investments specific to improve Toyota's productivity. The four factors concerning supplier relationships: sales revenues; profitability (Return on Sales); the number of employees; and, the percentage of supplier's equity held by the automaker can be used to compare relationships in different manufacturers (Kim and Michell, 1999).

The Japanese manufacturers also involve the first tier suppliers in co-design activities. Indeed, when western OEMs (Original equipment manufacturers) have tried to emulate Japanese settings, they have frequently failed to apply the *keiretsu* logic, a mix of arm's length and long-term relationships on the basis of supplier segmentation (Zirpoli and Caputo, 2002 cite Dyer, 1998).

5. FUTURE ACTION PLAN:

The western auto manufacturers should probably create a hybrid structure where the suppliers and the relationship with them should be segregated into two types:

    a. Suppliers supplying components which are produced by few numbers of suppliers, Chrysler should partner with them and involve them in co-design activities and nourish long term relationships.

    b. Suppliers producing components which are produced

by a large number of suppliers, in this case Chrysler should create a competition among the suppliers. The reason for including competition is that it is a cultural aspect of USA which is to cherish competition more than relationship.

The advantages of this hybrid model are shown below:

i.   The suppliers of type (a) will feel obliged and try to overcome internal problems and cater to the buyer.
ii. Creating competition among suppliers is not totally a bad approach; it's just that it is slightly short term orientated. But in case of (b), there are more options to fall back in case of crisis.
iii. This approach has taken into account the best of East (partnership) and West (competition).
iv. This variation of Japanese approach is created to suit the Western culture and outlook.

But eventually competition should be fully eliminated and partnership should be embraced and pursued in order to sustain in the market and promote the idea that as a matter of fact business and ethics can be together.

6. CONCLUSION:

We can't expect a life of Alice like in "Alice in Wonderland" where a Cheshire cat appears and baffles and amuses us and fades out with a grin. We have to face reality and accept the truth the way it is and not the way we like it to be. However big or small, nobody is invincible at all times and failure or success is temporary and success comes as long as "you could walk long enough".

REFERENCES

Bluesky Interactive (2008). *Chrysler history.*

http://www.cheapchryslerjeep.co.uk/chrysler.shtml

Hyde C. K. (2003). *Riding the Roller Coaster: A History of the Chrysler Corporation.* Detroit: Wayne State University Press, 2003
http://books.google.co.uk/books?id=aQhTq18vi7AC&pg=PA333
&dq=short+history+of+chrysler&sig=DHORJPrfGyDhIDQ0XU
H1elbqoTs#PPP1,M1

Kaplan R., Norton D.P. (2005). The Office of Strategy Management. *Strategic Finance.* 87(4), pg. 8, 4 pgs http://proquest.umi.com/pqd
web?index=2&did=911491181&SrchMode=1&sid=2&Fmt=4&
VInst=PROD&VType=PQD&RQT=309&VName=PQD&TS=
1211282378&clientId=28275

Kim J.B., Michell P. (1999). Relationship marketing in Japan: the buyer-supplier relationships of four automakers. *Journal of Business & Industrial Marketing.* 14(2), pp: 118-130 http://www.
emeraldinsight.com/Insight/ViewContentServlet?Filename=Publi
shed/EmeraldFullTextArticle/Articles/0800140203.html

Lardenoije E.J.H., Raaij E.M.V., Weele A.J.V. (2005). Performance Measurement Models and Purchasing: Relevance still lost. *Researches in purchasing and supply chain management.* March 20-23, pp 687-97 http://www.arjanvanweele.com/39/assets/File/
Publication articles/Publications conferences/Lardenoije.Raaij.
IPSERA.PerformanceManagement.EtAl2005ho.pdf

Morath E. (2008). *TRW strike in Windsor shuts down Chrysler.*
http://www.detnews.com/apps/pbcs.dll/article?AID=/20080229/
AUTO01/802290331/1148

Neely A. (1999). The performance measurement revolution: why now and what next? International Journal of Operations & Production Management. 19(2), 205-228. http://www.

emeraldinsight.com/Insight/ViewContentServlet?Filename=Publi
shed/EmeraldFullTextArticle/Articles/0240190206.html

Neely A., Adams C. (2002). *The Performance Prism (Image)*. http://
www.performance-measurement.net/news-detail.asp?nID=31

Neely A., Mills J., Platts K., Richards H., Gregory M., Bourne M.,
Kennerley M., (2000). Performance measurement system design:
developing and testing a process-based approach. *International
Journal of Operations & Production Management.* 20(10), 1119-1145
http://www.emeraldinsight.com/Insight/ViewContentServlet?Filen
ame=Published/EmeraldFullTextArticle/Articles/0240201001.html

Paul Arveson (1998). *Balanced Score Card (Image)*. http://www.
jiscinfonet.ac.uk/infokits/analytical-tools/scorecard

Saad M., Patel B. (2006). An investigation of supply chain
performance measurement in the Indian automotive sector.
An International Journal. 13 (1/2), pp: 36-53 http://www.
emeraldinsight.com/Insight/ViewContentServlet?Filename=Publi
shed/EmeraldFullTextArticle/Articles/1310130103.html

Zirpoli F., Caputo M. (2002). The nature of buyer-supplier
relationships in co-design activities - The Italian auto industry
case. *International Journal of Operations & Production Management.*
22(12), pp: 1389-1410 http://www.emeraldinsight.com/Insight/V
iewContentServlet?Filename=Published/EmeraldFullTextArticle/
Articles/0240221205.html

CHAPTER – II

LEAN MANAGEMENT IN FORD
INTRODUCTION:

Who likes rules and regulations? Not me or anyone I know. But what if there are rules and regulations for you to follow, which will definitely succeed in your work? That's what the Quality Management and Lean Management is all about. These are set of rules for you to follow which are time-tested and definitely successful. Why is it called lean management? Because in lean management we try to do "More" with "Less". According to Womack (2008), founder and chairman of the non-profit Lean Enterprise Institute (LEI), the term "lean production" refers to "A complete business system for organizing and managing product development, operations, suppliers, customer relations, and the overall enterprise that requires less human effort, less space, less capital, less material, and less time to make products with fewer defects to precise customer desires, compared with traditional management". We are going to see how lean management was adopted and implemented in Ford Motor Co.

HISTORY AND INITIAL STRATEGY OF FORD:

A young mechanic and entrepreneur named Henry Ford was trying to design a car that was easy to manufacture and repair. He had a vision: a simple, cheap and durable car for common people. After several bankruptcies he finally succeeded in 1908 with Model T. Over the next decade Ford invented a system that could turn out quality cars at lower and lower prices (Dennis, 2005).

His concept of mass production has now become almost obsolete. But it was an astonishing feat at that time. Every year, cars got cheaper and better. Henry's manufacturing innovations are legendary (Dennis, 2005):

- Standard gauging, faithfully used.
- Design for ease of assembly and part interchange ability.
- Fewer moving parts in engines and sub-systems.

- The assembly line.

Fordism and Mass Production:

"Fordism" was coined in about 1916 to describe Henry Ford's successes in the automobile industry. From raw materials to a complete car, Ford made everything in his own company. This kind of vertical integration was adopted for 2 main reasons. One, he had perfected the mass production techniques, and was able to achieve economies of scale by doing everything within the company. The next reason is because of the processing capabilities of that time and Ford's scepticism towards finance and accounting, it was found to be advantageous to directly supervise the coordination of raw material and components through the production process (Chandler, 1977). Total vertical integration, had its own challenges of organizing huge numbers of activities and employees. Employees have to be recruited, sorted out and fitted in the hierarchical ladder from Workers to staff specialists to middle managers.

Problems of Mass Production:

There were some problems with mass production, they believed in the trade off in quality in order to save costs. This is represented in the graph below:

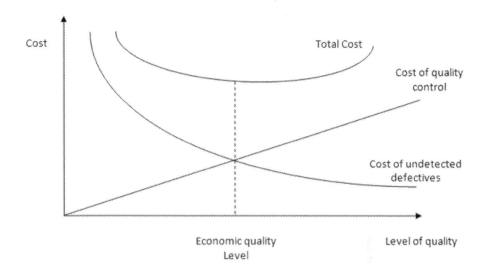

**Figure 2.1: Mass production approach to cost of quality
(Lamming, 1993)**

The straight line marked the 'cost of quality' implies that the level of quality (measured by reject rates, etc.) improves, as number of inspectors, amount of equipment, etc. increases. The notion of economic quality level – often expressed operationally as accepted quality level (AQL) – is based upon trade off between this cost and the cost of defective work which is not detected by inspection. It is traditionally assumed for the diagram that only these two costs exist; thus the total cost is the sum of two (Lamming, 1993):

The mass production ethic caused people to think in terms of strengthening traditional quality efforts (extra inspectors, measuring machines, better rectification process, etc.) rather than using lateral approaches such as employee involvement and 'quality is free' (Lamming, 1993).

FORDISM TO LEAN PRODUCTION:

The vertical integration developed by Ford served the mass production industry well during the years when the market accepted what it was offered. But complacency took over, after the mid of 1970s the good business changed drastically (Foreman-Peck *et al*, 1995).

The shock to the automotive assembly industry was severe: the impact upon suppliers was immense. Relationships between the two suffered as a result. By the turn of the decade, the supply industry was in dire straits, a situation had to occur and it took the form of better relationships – or at least the public affirmation of this intention by the assemblers.

Since the late 1970s the car manufacturers have converged on similar strategies aimed at managing the transition from mass production to lean production. All had sought to improve and accelerate their design capability, while also lowering their break-even point. The supply chain from component manufacturers to vehicle assemblers experienced massive restructuring.

Quality Process Path:

The path travelled by Ford Motor Co. in the context of quality process from the 1970s to the current date is shown below:

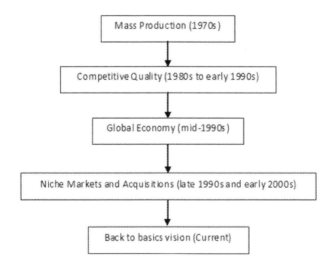

Figure 2.2: Quality Process Path of Ford

Back To Basics Vision (Current):

By saying back to basics, the management of Ford Motor Co. say that they want to go back to competitive quality of the 1980s on the context of Management, Manufacturing, Engineering and Suppliers. It can be described as below (Smith, 2005):

1. Management: Emphasis on People and Knowledge, Teamwork, Processes, Systems Thinking, Cost/Profit, Eco-Effective design.

2. Manufacturing: Q1, Basic Quality system, Variability reduction using SPC and DoE, Process Improvement, Lean/Flexible Manufacturing, Six Sigma Problem Solving, Regular Senior Management quality meetings.

3. Engineering: Q1 Program for Engineering, A disciplined method to implement "prevent" quality methods tied to reward and recognition (Design for Six Sigma), Training and software on powerful, cutting edge methods of TRIZ (The Theory of Inventive Problem Solving) and axiomatic design.

4. Suppliers: Longer Term collaborative partnerships operating in a lean value stream.

Difference between Mass and Lean Production:

Let's see what Mann (2005) has got to say about the difference between the old way of mass production and the lean production which is shown below:

Mass Production: Personally Focused Work Practices	Lean Production: Process Focused Work Practices
Independent	Interdependent, closely linked
Self-paced work and breaks	Process-paced work, time as a discipline
"Leave me alone"	"I work as a part of team"
"I get my own parts and supplies"	In and out cycle work are separated and standardized

"We do whatever it takes to get the job done; I know whom I can rely on at crunch time"	There's a defined process for pretty much everything; follow the process
"I define my own methods"	Methods are standardised
Results are the focus, do whatever it takes	Process focus is the path to consistent results
"Improvement is someone else's job; it's not my responsibility"	Maintenance problems should be foreseen as part of the production processes.
"Maintenance takes care of the equipment when it breaks; it's not my responsibility"	Improvement is the job for everyone
Managed by the pay or bonus system	Managed by performance to expectations

TOOLS OF LEAN MANAGEMENT

Dolcemascolo (2006) describes the various tools of lean management as Value Stream Mapping and the seven wastes that are to be eliminated in the value stream and the five Ss to implement lean management in a production. Those tools are explained below:

Value Stream Mapping:

To understand what value stream mapping is, we need to know what value is, what value stream is and what the significance of value stream mapping is. Value is defined as what a customer is willing to pay for. Value stream is the set of actions and process that takes to deliver the product to the customer. The steps involved in the value stream are a combination of actions that have value and those that do not have value. The idea is to eliminate those actions which create no value, and those that are not necessary because of the technological needs. People often confuse value stream mapping and process mapping. The difference is that process mapping is just about the process, but value stream mapping is about mapping the information (feedback) and product flow for a given value stream. The mapping involves visualization of both current state and future state (Dolcemascalo, 2006).

Seven Wastes:

People who have exposure to lean thinking know about "The Seven Wastes" which was defined by former Chief Engineer of Toyota Mr. Taiichi Ohno. He observed the shop floor activities and found the seven wastes of production and Mr Womack had added an eighth waste and they are (Dolcemascalo, 2006):

1. **Overproduction** – When the number of products produced is more than the number of products needed then it is overproduction. This is mainly caused by poor flow of information between facilities.

2. **Transportation** – Improper supplier selections may cause unnecessary transportation and which must be avoided by selecting the supplier/facility properly.

3. **Unnecessary Inventory** – Inventory becomes unnecessary again because of poor information flow and batch processing. Sometimes, redundant inventory is held by the supplies and their customers which need to be exposed.

4. **Inappropriate Processing** – This refers to process not being appropriate, which ends up in rework. This can also be due to wrong process and/or wrong supplier.

5. **Waiting** – Machines may have to wait and also product may wait which needs to be eliminated by proper feedback.

6. **Excess Motion** – This is the production personnel's motion and their work area, in order to reach out to locate tools, materials, etc.

7. **Defects** – This refers to both product defect and information defect. The product defect may cause excess of inventory and rework.

8. **Underutilization of Employees' Minds/Ideas** – It refers to employees, suppliers and customer to leverage their know-how in the context of manufacturing processes, information processing, and product design.

Five Ss: Created in Japan, the 5S's are: seiri, seiton , seiso, seiketsu, and shitsuke. Translated to English, we have (Dolcemascalo, 2006):

- **Sort** - remove all items from the workplace that are NOT needed for current production.

- **Set in Order** - arranging needed items so that they are easy to find and put away. Items used often are placed closer to employee.

- **Shine** - making sure everything is clean, functioning, and ready to go.

- **Standardize** - the method you use to maintain the first 3S's.

- **Sustain** - making a habit of properly maintaining correct procedures.

LEAN CHANGES IN FORD:

There are two different changes that happened in Ford Motor Co. in order to convert from Mass Production to Lean Production. They are:

1. *Technological Changes:* Introduction of Automated Storage and Retrieval System (AS/RS).
2. *Relationship Changes:* Aligned Business Framework (Partnership with the Suppliers).

We shall delve into the general principles, models and concepts related to these changes and relate it to what was implemented in For Motor Co.

TECHNICAL CHANGES:

Before analysing the technical change in Ford, let's see the different academic models available for the technical changes in a company and then relate it to the changes that happened in Ford.

Evolution of Models for Technical Change:

It is necessary to consider the nature of technical change, and the likely manner in which it will manifest itself. The search of origins of technical change and its development has centred upon a basic argument on causality which may be reduced to a simple representation as shown below (Lamming, 1993):

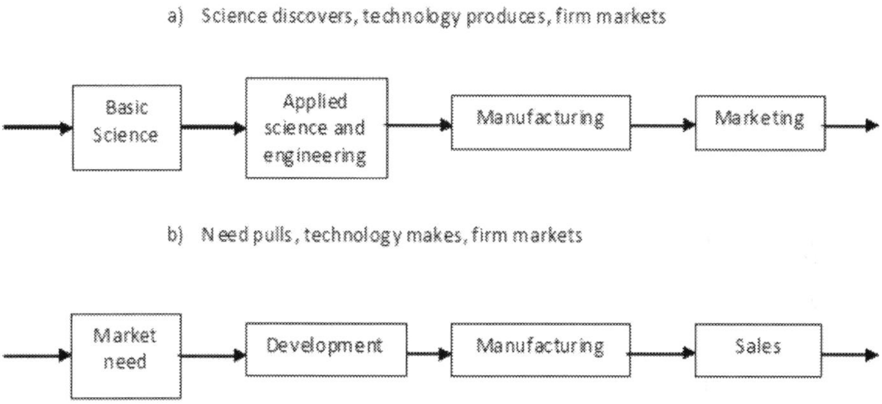

a) Science discovers, technology produces, firm markets

| Basic Science | → | Applied science and engineering | → | Manufacturing | → | Marketing |

b) Need pulls, technology makes, firm markets

| Market need | → | Development | → | Manufacturing | → | Sales |

Figure 2.3: Basic Causality Model for technical change

As you can see, the old models lack the interactive nature of the market and the innovation. This was later taken up by Schumpeter who created an interactive model, where there were small, innovative technical firms and large entrepreneurial, mature firms. The technology based firm are ones who can create and have sufficient resources to pursue the development of original or semi-original product ideas from scientific concepts to working prototype. This output is sold to the entrepreneurial firms who make it a commercial reality. This concept is shown below (Lamming, 1993):

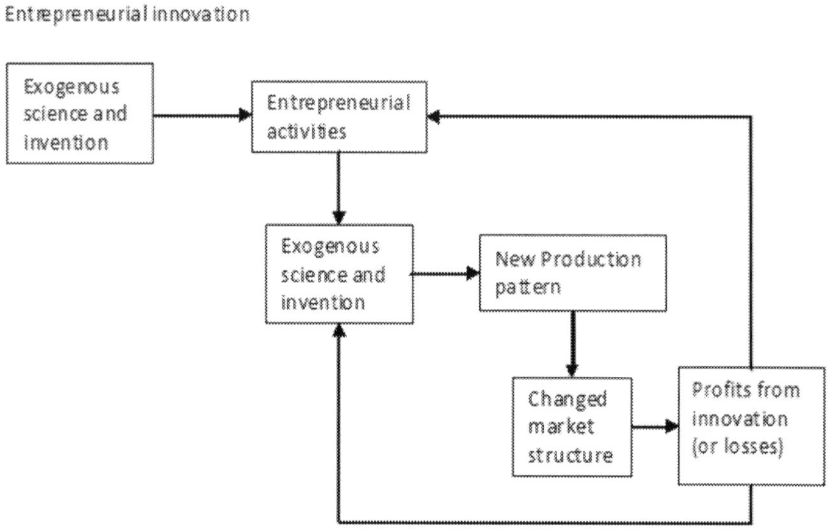

Entrepreneurial innovation

Figure 2.4: Schumpeter's first model of technical change

This is based on Schumpeter's assumption that innovation cannot be managed, so it has to be dealt with an external body. But later he came up with the second model which is based on the assumption that innovation can be managed.

The second model acknowledges the profound role of internal R&D to the firm. The role of independent inventors (exogenous innovation) is still noted. The blending of science and technology and innovative investment and market was once not very popular, but now it is more continuous and intimate.

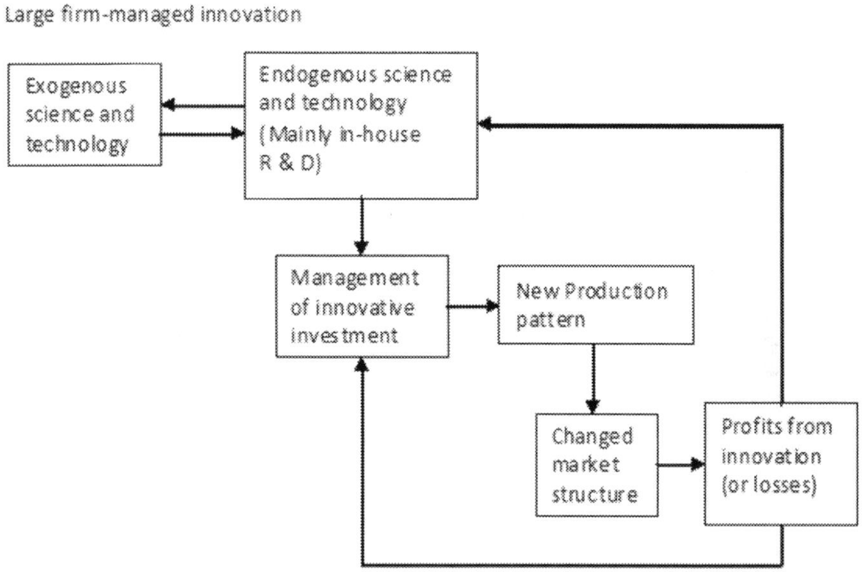

Large firm-managed innovation

Figure 2.5: Schumpeter's second model of managed innovation

The model of Schumpeter was challenged by Schmookler (1950s and 60s), who concluded that innovation followed market demand, and not the vice versa. This model is shown below, as discussed, the market demand is the start of innovative technical change (Lamming, 1993).

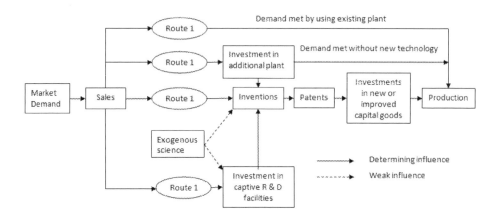

Figure 2.6: Schmookler's model of technical change

The modern firms are mostly a combination of both Schumpeter and Schmookler. This idea was converted to an interactive model by Rothwell and Zegveld in 1985 which is shown below ((Lamming, 1993) :

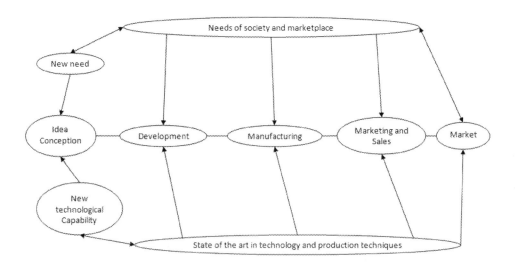

Figure 2.7: Rothwell and Zegveld interactive model of technical change.

Technology Change in Ford:

Ford came up with an idea of automating its manufacturing of cars and mounted its first automated storage and retrieval system (AS/RS) in 1994. The system provides an option of changing the build order of the cars by providing an accumulating buffer before the parts proceed down the line.

Before the adoption of AS/RS, Ford used to send out a broadcast message to local suppliers for all parts required for scheduled assembly. This pressurises the suppliers to make certain that the parts arrive on time; otherwise the production line could potentially be held up.

Also Ford had to hold the inventory in-house for up to 2 days which is quite significant. After the automation, the system provides an accumulation point which allows the workers to change build order depending on the supplies received. This reduced the on-hand inventory from 2 days to 2 hours.

The technical change model of Rothwell and Zegveld is used to analyse the technical change that happened in Ford. The boxes and titles of their model are retained and adapted with changes specific to Ford are added in the relevant boxes about Ford.

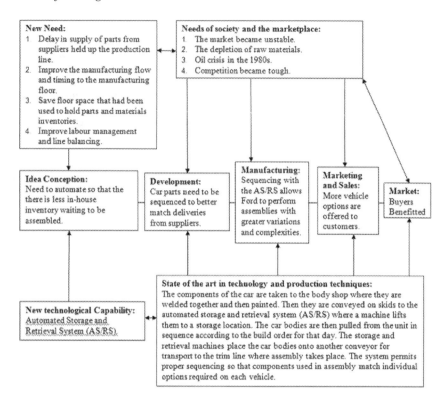

Figure 2.8: Adaptation of Rothwell and Zegveld interactive model of technical change to the technical change in Ford.

Benefits for Ford and Its Customers:

The AS/RS system has allowed Ford to improve its manufacturing stream and timing to the manufacturing floor, save factory floor space that had been used to hold parts and materials inventories, and improve labour Management and line balancing. Now, there are fewer inventories in the plant, it is easier to make line changes and engineering redesigns. This kind of sequencing process helps change the labour schedule according to the convenience. For example, it requires more personnel and workers to build a convertible than a standard sedan. By using the flexible sequence planning, labour can be better balanced. This also helps in concentrating on the complex details which a build needs and create improvement in quality (Maloney, 2002).

ALIGNED BUSINESS FRAMEWORK:

Ford Motor Co. came up with a single mission of sustained profitability which can be achieved with a new "Aligned Business Framework" program which aims to align buyers, suppliers, designers and assembly personnel. The apparent goal is to reduce the suppliers from 2,500 to 1,000 and to eventually halve the annual costs of procuring materials and distributing internally. The top management says that they want to operate on a supply chain management system that delivers in a fashion which is disciplined and comes to market in a faster time (Stundza, 2006).

Adoption of "Six Sigma":

At the beginning of the 21st century, Ford had to start improving the quality and reliability of the products. Since it adopted the processes of 'Six Sigma' for quality improvement, wastage was eliminated which ended in a lot of savings, the necessity for after purchase warranty service was significantly reduced and the customer satisfaction rose to new heights (Smith 2005).

The statistic shows the warranty services work had reduced to 27 percent 2001 to 2003 which is really astonishing. The people would definitely not feel happy about buying a new car that needs to be repaired soon after the purchase. The customers want quality and don't like that idea of giving the manufacturer chances to get things right (Smith, 2005).

Way Forward:

Ford's "Way Forward" plan is all about doing more with less which was advertised. They had to close 14 plants and lay off 30,000 workers. A comprehensive plan was drafted to reduce the time for development of product by 6 to twelve months and to transform North American

Assembly plants into flexible manufacturing operations. This should be supported by various innovative new-product developments and purchasing systems. The management does not believe that job cuts are the way to growth, they believe in innovation. That means innovating internally in design, in quality, in safety, in environmental impact and in production (Book Review, 2005).

Improving the Global Buy:

Ford buys production parts from the suppliers (more than 2500 worldwide) which are worth of $70 billion dollars per year. Ford had a policy that encouraged leaning on suppliers for the sake of annual price reductions. The company had a business model that reinforced this behaviour through a system of employee evaluations and bonuses for cost reductions. But this kind of contentious relationships with suppliers did not really reduce the costs sufficient enough. This business model had a problem in the industry. It was not working effectively for both the suppliers and the company. When the suppliers are financially stressed, there were shocks in commodity prices, problems in quality and issues in cost, then there probably is a better approach (Tundza, 2006). So, the head of management championed the Aligned Business Framework, a best practices approach of partnering with suppliers to cut costs.

Benefits of Aligned Business Framework:

The intention of the program is to create an environment between Ford and a select family of suppliers where innovative ideas can emerge, and then be incubated, evaluated and incorporated into the company's products. This program also helps to build good relationship with a group of suppliers who are more competent, and more financially stable suppliers on a long term basis. The time tested processes and strong and stable suppliers help to deliver innovation, high quality and low costs (Tundza, 2006).

Innovation in Relationships:

The Ford Motor Co. also incorporated innovation in the supply chain excellence system by introducing two-in-a-box "matched pairs" consisting of one employee from the production purchasing operation of Ford, The Americas and the employee from the engineering department of Ford Motor Co. have to work with preferred suppliers to improve sourcing and delivery. While one employee looked into the external issues like to directly interact with the drivers who can give the supplier issues and the other employee looked into the internal issues of cost estimation and material recovery to improve the relationships. At the end of the day, they merge their data to get the benefit of suppliers' first-class technology. When it comes to relationships, people tend to concentrate only on external people and lose the relationships within the organization, and sometimes they may indulge too much in the internal relationships, that they lose concentration on the outside world. But here, both are taken care with a perfect balance, now it all depends on how well the two people interact, co-ordinate and share information.

The program also came up with some projects for assessing the suppliers, which includes extensive annual reviews of parts suppliers, which are available to all car making organizations. This evaluation is based on 11 financial and non-financial metrics by which the buyers can judge the potential suppliers. Also a five-year supplier training plan is offered which will cover the areas of corporate social responsibility

Benefits of Improving Relationships:

Automotive analysts believe that this policy of partnering with suppliers creates a win-win situation: Ford obtains premium technology and cost cuts from the suppliers, and suppliers get long-term commitments that will enable better forecasting and planning. In the new Framework agreements with some preferred suppliers, Ford is promising more collaborative relationships marked by longer-term agreements, greater sourcing volume, and upfront payments for engineering and development work. Preferred suppliers selected for the plan will be those identified as the ones which are technically innovative and committed to quality, cost and delivery goals. (Tundza, 2006).

ANALYSIS OF SEVEN WASTES IN FORD:

The value stream mapping is in place especially in the information sharing with the supplier and changing the process accordingly and the seven wastes in the context of Ford are described below:

1. Overproduction: It requires a lot of courage to cut down the production in the unpredictable consumer market. But Toyota is supposed to have done it and hence it is advisable for Ford also to follow suit.

2. Waiting: Because of the proper relation management with the suppliers and the deployment of Automatic Storage and Retrieval System (AS/RS), the waiting has been totally eliminated.

3. Transporting: This also been eliminated because of the AS/RS and a single facility for manufacturing.

4. Inappropriate processing: A proper process is in place in terms of both production and manufacturing.

5. Unnecessary Inventory: Since waiting has been eliminated, the unnecessary inventory is fairly reduced, but the over production, may cause some unnecessary inventory.

6. Unnecessary motion: Because of Aligned Business Framework the internal and external relationships are handled by separate individuals. This could reduce the unnecessary motion.

7. Defects: Though not totally eliminated, the number of complaints has reduced drastically. They should aim at eliminating it totally and be synonymous to quality like Toyota.

8. Underutilization of Employees: The employees are being used effectively especially after the mass lay-off. Though, mass lay-off might end up in losing some potential employees, the attitude should hopefully be for better.

From the information available we can believe that all the 5Ss are in place in Ford.

So, the action plan in terms of lean management for future for Ford is to eliminate wastes due to overproduction, reduce the defects to zero and utilize employees effectively.

EMPLOYEE EMPOWERMENT:

Any company which does not concentrate on its employee's empowerment cannot survive for long. This is true for Ford, the company has been able to achieve higher commitment from the employees and the managers' capabilities were improved through various development processes. The UAW (United Auto Workers) together with Ford Employment Development and Training Program (EDTP) joined hands with Ford's own managerial development process and has helped to create a more effective corporate. These two activities provided the initiative for a more participative culture and also revitalised the global competitiveness (Denton, 1994).

Ford started operating training and development for employees all through their work life. It starts with selection and recruitment and continues until retirement. There are five track goals that Ford concentrates on (Denton, 1994)

- Understand core company values, practices, policies and guidelines;
- Learn general business, strategic and technical skills;
- Adopt functional/ professional knowledge and skills;
- Awareness of community, societal and governmental, by involvement and knowledge;
- Practise Individual motivation and personality development.

There are specific programs offered for not just hourly paid workers, but also for salaried employees and managers.

FUTURE ACTION PLAN:

The keys to success in future for Ford would include:

- Innovation in the fundamental approach
- Clarity in the Systems Thinking
- Strong Leadership
- A flair for strategy
- Recognition of the practical limits on resources.

The industry need to accept the fact that resources are depleting every day and we need to search for substitutes for the raw materials. For this the industry should look beyond its own industry. It is probably out there, but we just don't know yet. So, the automobile industry should unite together, create a R&D team for the research of substitute products and get benefitted mutually.

CONCLUSION:

The leanness can become successful for a company if the company is able to understand that the true potential of becoming lean exists inherent to the company and is dynamic in nature. It has to sense the needs and changes of the industry and update its scope, potential and content. This can be achieved by understanding the evolutionary process of the leanness and the various stages of its existence.

For those who don't like rules and regulations and want freedom, freedom without rules does not make sense and might end up in serious problems. Everything from how we accept rules and regulations and then innovate upon them depends on attitude within us. If you want to break the rules, first you will have to learn them only then will you know the problems and the scope.

REFERENCES

Author not mentioned (2005), Ford drives ahead with quality control - Morals and ethics of delivering reliability (Book Review). *Strategic Direction.* 21(10), 18-21

Dennis, Pascal (2005), *Andy & Me – Crisis Transformation on the Lean Journey,* New York: Productivity

Denton, D. K. (1994) Empowerment through Employee Involvement and Participation – Ford's Development and Training Programs. *Empowerment in Organizations.* 2(2), 22-28

Dolcemascolo, D. (2004). Seven Wastes of the Extended Value Stream. Available: http://www.emsstrategies.com/dd120104article1.html. Last accessed 7 Mar 2008

Foreman-Peck, J., Bowden, S., McKinlay, A. (1995), *The British Motor Industry,* New York: Manchester University

Lamming, Richard (1993), *Beyond Partnership – Strategies for Innovation and Lean Supply,* Hertfordshire: Prentice Hall

Maloney, David (2002) Ford takes control with AS/RS. *Modern Materials Handling.* 57(11), 29-30

Mann, David (2005), *Creating a Lean Culture – Tools to sustain Conversions,* New York: Productivity

Papadopoulou, T.C., Özbayrak, M. (2005) Leanness: experience from the journey to date. *Journal of Manufacturing Technology.* 16(7), 784-807

Smith, L. R. (2005) Back to the Future At Ford. *Quality Progress.* 38(3), 50-56

Thompson, Fred (year not known). *Fordism, Post-fordism and the flexible system of production* [online] Available from: http://www.willamette. edu/~fthompso/MgmtCon/Fordism_&_Postfordism.html [Accessed on 7th Mar 2008]

Tundza, Tom. (2006) Ford has a better idea. *Purchasing.* 135(12), pg. 49

Womack, P. James (2007), *Orlando Conference Advances Lean Management as Successor to Traditional Management*, [online] Available from:

http://www.pr-inside.com/orlando-conference-advances-lean-management-r427640.htmn [Accessed 7th Mar 2008]

CHAPTER – III

TOTAL QUALITY MANAGEMENT IN AMERICAN DEFENCE INDUSTRY

Good order is foundation of all good things.

– Oakland (1993) cites Edmund Burke (1791)

1. Introduction:
One of the US Army soldiers serving in Iraq says,

"We have no comprehension of the psychological cost of this war. I know kids in Iraq who killed themselves. I know kids that got killed. OK, that's apparently the price of doing business. But multiply me by 2 million. If I'm fairly high-functioning, what about the ones those aren't? They're going back to small-town America, and their families aren't going to know what to do with them. It's like, what do we do with Johnny now?" (Pavlina, 2007)

And many men and women like this soldier have to be taken care to succeed, and success itself is disputable as there has never been a consensus in the acceptance of the victory of the war. If it succeeds politically or military wise it probably fails in humanitarian basis. But men are still willing to accept the military service for various reasons and they have to be taken care, be it any army, American or Iraqi or Russian or Afghan or Indian. The intention is to discuss TQM in US Army and help others use it as reference for other Armies or other Industries.

2. History of American Army:
The American Army has evolved and undergone various historical stages along with social, political and economic development of United States. Its history can be divided into three important periods the colonial, the continental expansion and the overseas operations. The colonial

period which spans from 1607-1775 was when the colonial American defended the settlers especially England in eliminating the French from North America. This is the period when the England military was transplanted with military of England and they entered into the New World. The next era is the continental expansion from 1775-1898 in which the military participated both in the independence and the consolidation of the present geographical area by winning important territories, in avoiding internal destruction, policing, governing and exploring vast regions of the western part. The nation was formed based on the new concepts of individual freedom and representative government and played a vital role in establishing, maintaining and expanding the nation. In the third period which is 1898 to present the American Army has promoted peace successfully and sometimes unsuccessfully around the four corners of the world and is still retaining its pride (Centre of Military History, 2001).

3. Total Quality Management (TQM):

In general TQM is not just about making the manufacturer detect the problems rather than the customer, it is much more than that. TQM involves first recognising a comprehensive approach and then implementing the approach so that the rewards are obtained. This approach of TQM improves flexibility, competitiveness and effectiveness of the whole organization. This involves planning, organizing and understanding each activity and depends on each individual at every level which is represented in the following diagram (Oakland, 1993):

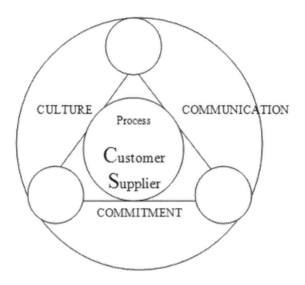

Figure 3.1: Components of TQM

The TQM has been emphasized by many management gurus for industries throughout the world among them are Philip B. Crosby and W Edward Deming who respectively defined the four absolutes and fourteen steps of quality improvement involved in TQM which is listed below:

Crosby has four absolutes of quality:

- Definition – conformance to requirements
- System – Prevention
- Performance standard – Zero Defects
- Measurement – price of non-conformance

"Deming's fourteen points for management:

1. Create constancy of purpose towards improvement of product and service.

2. Adopt the new philosophy. We can no longer live with commonly accepted levels of delays, mistakes, defective workmanship.
3. Cease dependence on mass inspection. Require, instead, statistical evidence that quality is built in.
4. End the practice of awarding the business on the basis of price tag.
5. Find problems. It is management's job to work continually on the system.
6. Institute modern methods of training in the job.
7. Institute modern methods of supervision of production workers. The responsibility of foremen must be changed from numbers to quality.
8. Drive out fear, so that everyone may work effectively for the company.
9. Break down barriers between departments.
10. Eliminate numerical goals, posters, and slogans for the work force asking for new levels of productivity without providing methods.
11. Eliminate work standards that prescribe numerical quotas.
12. Remove barriers that stand between the hourly worker and his right to pride of workmanship.
13. Institute a vigorous program of education and retraining.
14. Create a structure in top management that will push every day on the above thirteen points."

The techniques and methods used in TQM can be applied at every level and department of the organization. But whether TQM could be applied to a political industry like Army is an obvious question, but in the age of privatised war called terrorism, you'd rather be ahead. Moreover TQM cannot be detached from the human attitude and behaviour which is extremely vital in a defence industry. For example, enthusiasm to work is as important as skill of the employee in an industry (Grover *et al*, 2006). The human factors influencing the concept of TQM are represented by them below:

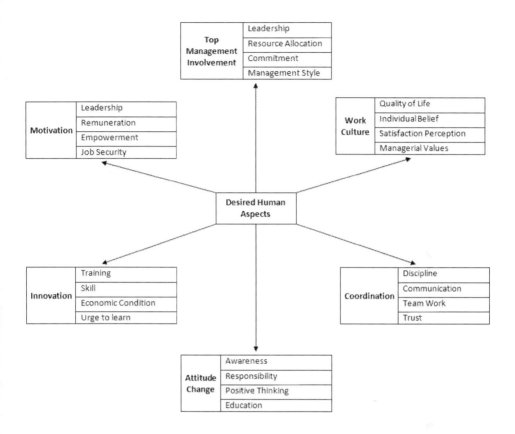

Figure 3.2: Human Factors Influencing TQM

The Department of Defence (DoD) defines quality in the following way:

"TQM is both a philosophy and a set of guiding principles that represent the foundation of a continuously improving organization. TQM is the application of quantitative methods and human resources to improve the material and services supplied to an organization and the degree to which the needs of the customer are met, now and in the future. TQM integrates fundamental management techniques, existing improvement efforts, and technical tools under a disciplined approach focused on continuous improvement."

4. TQM in US ARMY:

When soldiers are away from their home and in need of help, sometimes it is only fellow soldiers who can help and even on other times the only resort they have is technology and that kind of technology has to be confirmed for total quality. Technology has given up many times resulting in human losses in the recent space shuttle launches. So, every little detail has to be under inspection and testing and should be managed for total quality.

4.1 DoD Initiative:

The Department of Defence of United States instituted the master plan for TQM in 1988 that sets forth the concept of TQM, in accordance with goals, methodology and the actions which are specifically required. According to the plan devised in 1988, in addition to the defence program beginning to implement and improve continuously and manage with total quality, but also the top 25 contractors of defence have to be committed to the total quality before the end of the year 1992. Because of this program the 25 contractors were not just encouraged but were forced to implement TQM program which is proprietary and also equally rigorous. (Pitman *et al,* 1994).

The contractors of DoD who are its suppliers were motivated by this initiative to adopt TQM and the suppliers began to study the new process which is quality oriented to run their businesses, develop products, services and also manage the human resources. Traditionally the defence contracts have been allocated in terms of minimum performance criteria and competitiveness in price, and because there was a short term lag in buying products and services there was insufficient incentive given for quality improved products and processes prior to 1989 in the defence system (Pitman *et al,* 1994).

The contractors are expected to meet the following four criteria in order to win a contract with the defence system (Pitman *et al,* 1994):

- The supplier must be customer-driven and also responsive to customers.

- The company, at all times should ensure that it anticipates, meets and exceeds quality expectations of the customers.

- The company should demonstrate that quality is embedded not just in products but in all of its processes.

- The supplier's philosophy and process about TQM should have the participation of each and every employee of the company

4.2 **Comparison of old and New View** (Pitman *et al,* 1994):

Traditional View	New View
Productivity and quality are conflicting goals.	Productivity gains are achieved through quality improvements.
Quality defined as conformance to specifications or standards.	Quality is correctly defined as requirements satisfying user needs.
Quality is measured by degree of conformance.	Quality is measured by continuous process improvement and user satisfaction.
Quality is achieved through intensive product inspection.	Quality is determined by product design and is achieved by effective control techniques.
Quality is a separate function and focused on evaluating production.	Quality is apart if every function in all phases of the product cycle.
Workers are blamed for poor quality.	Management is responsible for quality.
Supplier relations are short-term and cost-oriented.	Supplier relations are long-term and quality oriented.

4.3 **Problems in implementing TQM:**

When TQM was implemented, two major difficulties arose which were (1) How to learn to define a problem (2) How exactly the process should be measured. The employees like the worker, engineers and customers often agree that there is a problem, but at the same time they have some disagreements regarding what the problem is. The major step towards solving a problem is to define the problem. This varied discretions made them to use charts about cause and effect, functional quality deployment, and also they came up with team sessions to improve the process of defining a problem (Pitman *et al*, 1994).

The next obstacle is how to measure processes. It was relatively easy to measure the processes of external and internal customers, it was much more difficult to define and measure intangible processes of engineering and administration. Each of the departments finally agreed on the number of processes that needs to be measured. The transition to new methods faced some difficulties as some people wanted to use the traditional methods which also was a problem for benchmarking across departments. When some benchmarks were not known, standards were defined to provide future criterion which are to be used to measure against. In spite of showing progress, the defence system needs many improvements in the area of processes.

The inspectors are deployed on-site at all times at the supplier's facility and are involved in all stages of manufacturing. These inspectors are considered to be part of the quality process team and they work jointly with the company's processes to improve the quality processes. However the Vice president of the supplier feel that the inspectors are sometimes an interruption as they tend to concentrate more on solving small problems than concentrating important ones which may demand more time (Pitman *et al*, 1994).

In order to motivate and reward employees a gain-sharing program was introduced for quality improvement. A committee set the goals and the performance of employees is tracked using the bulletin boards within the company. Also awards for excellence were added for both personal and group recognition. The suggestions of the employees were also handled by a system called "Error Cause Removal" system or ECR. A TQM administrator was made responsible for collecting and forwarding suggestions to a cross-functional committee for review. The feasibility of the suggestion is evaluated and necessary action is taken within 30 days. Because of quality improvements many benefits have been achieved in the supplier's site. The customer loyalty increases, scrap was reduced, labour costs were lowered, higher margins of profit were achieved and the productivity was increased. The quality program has become an ongoing practice in operations and strategies (Pitman *et al,* 1994).

4.4 Conformance of TQM in US Army:

Now let's analyse if the TQM concepts are conformed in the US Army we will use Crosby's four absolutes and Deming's fourteen points.

4.4.1. Crosby's four absolutes of quality:

S. No.	Crosby's Four Absolutes	Whether Conformed or not?
1	Definition – conformance to requirements	Yes. The requirements standards are decided by large corporate sites like AT & T and Intel.
2	System – Prevention	Yes. Pentagon shifted from testing the product to testing the product and also the process
3	Performance standard – Zero Defects	Yes. An 'Error Cause Removal (ECR)' System was introduced.
4	Measurement – price of non-conformance	Not fully. From the information available there seems to be some kind anomalies in terms measurements and identification of problems. Proper standards have to be in place. Like in any group of thinking people there will be different perceptions and arguments and that's the reason the standards should be in place.

4.4.2. Deming's Fourteen points for management:

S. No.	Deming's fourteen points	Whether conformed or not?
1	Create constancy of purpose towards improvement of product and service.	Yes. The AT & T and Intel must be doing this.
2	Adopt the new philosophy. We can no longer live with commonly accepted levels of delays, mistakes, defective workmanship.	Yes. The initiation and transition have happened.
3	Cease dependence on mass inspection. Require, instead, statistical evidence that quality is built in.	Yes. The development and staff support for various statistical activities, such as quality functional deployment, statistical process control, etc. are provided.
4	End the practice of awarding the business on the basis of price tag.	Yes. The emphasis on quality remains.
5	Find problems. It is management's job to work continually on the system.	Not Fully. There still is trouble in defining the exact problem in hand.
6	Institute modern methods of training in the job.	Yes. The modern methods of training and education are in place.
7	Institute modern methods of supervision of production workers. The responsibility of foremen must be changed from numbers to quality.	Yes. Resident inspectors are on-site at all times at this contractor's manufacturing facility and are involved in all stages of manufacturing.
8	Drive out fear, so that everyone may work effectively for the company.	Yes. A new system to handle employee suggestions was also implemented.
9	Break down barriers between departments.	Not fully. The process area still needs improvement.
10	Eliminate numerical goals, posters, and slogans for the work force asking for new levels of productivity without providing methods.	Not fully. As mentioned above the process must be more detailed.
11	Eliminate work standards that prescribe numerical quotas.	Yes. Statistics are taken and used but used as only guidelines.

12	Remove barriers that stand between the hourly worker and his right to pride of workmanship.	Yes. Excellence awards were added for both personal and group recognition.
13	Institute a vigorous program of education and retraining.	Yes. The in-house training program comprised of 20 hours of classroom lectures and ten hours of outside work.
14	Create a structure in top management that will push every day on the above thirteen points.	Yes. Permanent train and support quality groups are available.

5. **Conclusion:** The intention is not to support any kind of war or violence against anybody in the world. As Mark Twain says,

"All war must be just the killing of strangers against whom you feel no personal animosity; strangers whom, in other circumstances, you would help if you found them in trouble, and who would help you if you needed it." - Mark Twain, "The Private History of the Campaign That Failed"

War cannot be stopped overnight because in that case it is very likely that it will return. War and its insanity have to be stopped over time by imparting the ethos of humanity and this is one step towards that.

REFERENCES:

CENTER OF MILITARY HISTORY (2001). AMERICAN MILITARY HISTORY. *[online]* http://www.history.army.mil/books/AMH/AMH-01.htm

Grover S., Agrawal V.P., Khan I.A. (2006). Role of human factors in TQM: a graph theoretic approach. *Benchmarking: An International Journal.* 13(4). pp 447-468 *[Available for Athens Users at]* http://www.emeraldinsight.com/Insight/ViewContentServlet?Filename=Publishe d/EmeraldFullTextArticle/Articles/1310130403.html

Oakland J.S. (1993). *Total Quality Management – The route to improving performance,* Oxford: Butterworth-Heinemann Ltd.

Pavlina S. (2007). Stories from Soldiers in Iraq. *[online]* http://www.stevepavlina.com/blog/2007/07/stories-from-soldiers-in-iraq/

Pitman G.A., Motwani J.G., Schliker D., (1994). Total Quality Management in the American Defence Industry - A Case Study. *International Journal of Quality & Reliability Management.* 11 (9). pp 101-108 *[Available for Athens Users at]* http://www.emeraldinsight.com/Insight/ViewContentServlet?Filename=Publishe d/EmeraldFullTextArticle/Articles/0400110907.html

MARKETING

CHAPTER – IV

MARKETING MODELS AND APPLICATION TO iPod

1. INTRODUCTION

In today's dynamic and shrunk world, developing and marketing successful products have become more and more difficult, for four important reasons (Smith and Swinyard, 1999):

a. Only one out of 60 product ideas reach the market. So, the investment in research is very high.

b. About 40%-90% of new products fail in the first year depending on the industry.

c. Due to increasing competition and discrimination from consumers, the new products have only half the life span of what it was ten years ago.

d. The development costs which include fragmented markets, very high research costs and capital shortages are mushrooming.

In this context, the survival of the fittest is the innovative Apple's iPod which has produced astounding success all over the world. The aim is to study three different marketing models and apply those models to the marketing of iPod. The three chosen models are "Boston Consulting Group (BCG) Matrix", Rogers' "Innovation Adoption Curve," and Kano's "Customer Satisfaction Model".

2. BOSTON CONSULTING GROUP MATRIX

The BCG Matrix or the portfolio matrix was originally suggested by Boston Consulting Group in the 1970s to prioritize a product portfolio of a company or department. This matrix helps for market analysis in terms of relative market share and market growth. Market Share is important in a commercial sector and it is advantageous to have higher share. Market Growth implies more opportunities for various activities (Nutton, 2007). There are four regions in the matrix namely Stars, Cash Cows, Problem Child or Question Mark and Dogs which is represented in the Figure 1.1. We shall study each of the four cells.

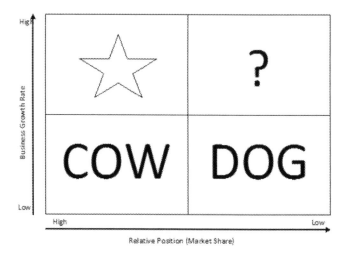

Figure 4.1: BCG Matrix

a) **Stars**

Products falling in this region have High Relative Market Share and High Growth Markets. The products that fall in this region needs heavy investment but will also generate high income. In course of time, the market growth will diminish and will have to move to Cash Cows (Walton, 2007). If the growth of the market slows down, the stars can move on to other quadrants depending on the gain or loss of market share. Losing market share will make it Dog and gaining market share will make it Cash Cow (Mayo, 2006). So, eventually the income from this product can be used to reinvest in some other product in the portfolio. To make this happen, investment should be made for the star product throughout the growth phase (Nutton, 2007).

b) **Cash Cows**

Cash Cow products are those with High market Share and slow

or negative growth. In these cases, the cash generated will exceed the reinvestment required to maintain the market share. This excess can be invested elsewhere in the portfolio. The Cash cows have to be safeguarded which in turn will fund the position in the market, fund R & D, pay for dividends, and subsidize higher growth products (Nutton, 2007). They generate both profit and cash (Walton, 2007).

c) **Problem Child**

This represents products with low market share and high market growths. This proportion suggests that the income is low and investment is high (Walton, 2007). These products may fail when sufficient cash is not available. The investment to gain more market share may become a liability. So, crucial decisions have to be made whether to invest or drop (Nutton, 2007).

d) **Dogs**

The dogs represent the quadrant with low market growth and low market share. These products often show accounting profit, but have to be reinvested in order to maintain the position, so it cannot help other products in the portfolio. Though the BCG recommends dropping the product, there are some questions that have to be answered. Is the product contributing any profits? What is the impact on other products if this is dropped? What is the impact on the overall brand? Do customers get attracted to the business? What about the competitors? Are they likely to leave? Can this dog be converted to cash cow? (Nutton, 2007)

Advantages of BCG Matrix

The BCG Matrix is easy to apply and a portfolio is set to be balanced if it contains a number of stars to grow and cows to generate cash. The advantages of this model is that it focuses on making a product profitable and also guides to develop strategies and growth of the portfolio on a long term basis. The graphic representation helps easy communication (Walton, 2007).

Limitations of BCG Matrix: It is a broad distinction that's being used, and also it is believed that good strategies can come from more than just market analysis. It is more scientific and in reality the decisions are subjective. The usage of terms like "cash cow" and "dog" are derogatory (Walton, 2007). The BCG matrix is less easy to apply and is based on the fact that growth can be achieved only with growing market share. But in reality competitive advantage can be achieved by advanced technology, quality, better customer services, geographical location and speed of response. It can also be that competitive edge can be gained by contraction rather than growth. Also, the BCG Matrix ranks only based on market growth and share, showing that short term profit is the only competitive advantage. For example dogs can be profitable and self sufficient (Nutton, 2007).

3. INNOVATION ADOPTION CURVE

The innovation adoption curve was found by Rogers in 1983, it was also called the Diffusion of Innovation Theory (DOI). The important paradigm of this theory is the decision process used by the potential adopters to select or reject a new technology. The stages involved in this process are found to be Knowledge, Persuasion, Decision, Implementation and Confirmation or Denial (Shockman, 2000 cites Rogers, 1983).

Figure 4.2: Process for selecting new technology

Rogers identified five different categories of innovation adopters:

a) **Innovators**

Brave people, pulling the change are the innovators and they form an important communication. About 2.5% of population belong to this category. They are also called "Venturesome" (Shockman, 2000).

b) **Early Adopters**

The people who belong to this category are respectable people, opinion leaders and try out new ideas, but in a careful way. They constitute 13.5% of the total population who are also called "Respectable" (Shockman, 2000).

c) **Early Majority**

In this category the people are thoughtful and careful but accepting change more quickly than the average. Approximately 34% of the population fall into this category and are also called "Deliberate" (Shockman, 2000).

d) **Late Majority**

The part of the population who are sceptical, and will use new ideas or products only when the majority starts using it is similar to Early Majority, 34% fall in this category those are also called "Sceptical" (Shockman, 2000). The early and late majority combined form 68% of the population and are the people who decide whether an innovation is a success or not.

e) **Laggards**

The traditional people who like to stick to old ways, critical towards new ideas and accept new ideas only if it has become main stream or tradition. About 16% belong to this category and are called "Traditional" (Shockman, 2000).

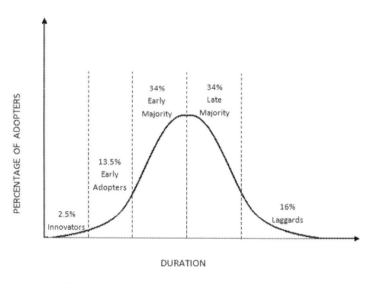

Figure 4.3: Innovation Adoption Curve

Advantages of innovation adoption curve

This curve helps us to remember that we need not aim at satisfying the mass, and would rather try to convince the innovators and early adopters. Also, the categories and percentages are useful to estimate the target consumers in order to find ways to communicate.

Limitations

The recent studies have shown that there is usually a gap between the innovators and early adopters (Shockman, 2000 cites Moore, 1991) and the crossing of that gap is not addressed by Rogers' model.

4. **CUSTOMER SATISFACTION MODEL**

The Kano's customer satisfaction model is used to measure the happiness of the client. Kano *et al.* (1984) considered six different categories of customer satisfaction of which three are highly influential.

a) Basic Factors (Must Haves, Dissatisfiers)

The minimum requirement of the product which the consumer would feel dissatisfied if they are not available and not exactly satisfied if they are available. These requirements are considered as prerequisites and usually taken for granted. These factors constitute the threshold for market entry. For example if the brakes in a car do not work it will cause high dissatisfaction to the customer (Sireli et. al., 2005).

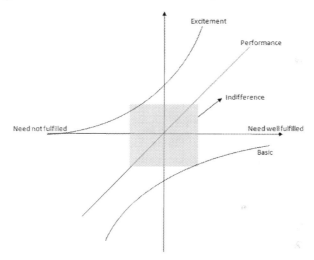

Figure 4.4: Customer Satisfaction Model

b) Performance Factors (One Dimensional)

The requirement of the product which the consumer would feel dissatisfied if they are not available and satisfied if they are available. Hence this representation is linear and symmetric in the graph. These are based on the explicit needs of the customers and the organizations can be competitive here. For example the mileage of a car can cause satisfaction if it is more and dissatisfaction when less (Sireli et. al., 2005).

c) Excitement Factors (Attractive, Satisfiers)

These are factors of product which causes satisfaction when available and not really dissatisfaction when not available. These factors take consumers by surprise and delight them. For example, lack of moon roof cannot cause dissatisfaction when not available. These factors can distinguish the company from the competitors (Sireli et. al., 2005).

There are three more factors which are not very influential:

d) Indifferent factors

The factors about which the customer do not care which falls on the centre of the graph. For example a cigarette lighter in a car (Sireli et. al., 2005).

e) Questionable factors

The factors which were found to be obtained because of wrong questions where incorrect response was received (Sireli et. al., 2005).

f) Reverse factors:

The customer expects the reverse of the factor that's available (Sireli et. al., 2005).

Advantages of Kano's Model

This is a unique and flexible model for gathering customer expectations. Traditionally customer satisfaction is analysed using surveys, questionnaires and interviews and a linear relation between the product performance and the customer satisfaction is assumed. However, in reality the customer satisfaction depends on the type of expectation. The different types of expectations about a product will have different type of customer satisfaction which is identified in this model (Sireli et. al., 2005).

Limitations

The Kano's model can only be used for the analysis of existing products, and not for new products which is very difficult to achieve. Also, the limitations are far lesser than the advantages (Jacowski, 2008).

5. **APPLE'S iPod**

Apple's success came about with compromises to meet the customer requirements and reach out to as many consumers as possible. After the unexpected introduction of iPod in October 2001, about 125,000 iPods were sold by the end of 2001. Until July 2002, the iPod was only meant for Mac machines, which was changed and PC versions were unveiled in 2003 and with improvements of USB cable in 2004. The sales moved from good to fantastic during that time. In August 2004, Apple announced sales of about 3.7 million iPods. Analysts report that iPod sales are 82% of all digital music players and 92% of all hard-drive based players; nearest hard drive competitor Creative has 3.7%. The various changes that were incorporated in the features of iPod from the first generation iPod to the fourth generation iPod and iPod mini are available in APPENDIX - I (Lloyd, 2004).

The chart of the sales of iPod is shown below:

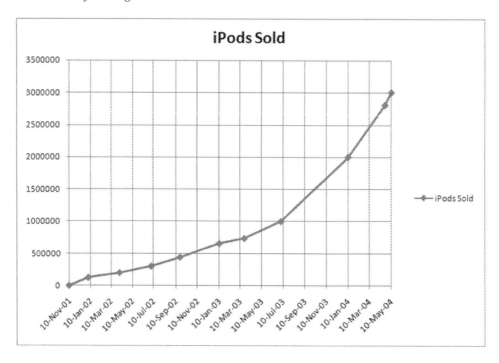

Figure 4.5: The iPods sold reaching 3 million in 2004

6. **BCG MATRIX FOR iPod**

The iPod was a radically new product, and took everyone by surprise. In a span of two years, the Apple's stock price has increased nearly 600 percent, which is attributed to the success of the iPod digital music player. Around three quarters of digital music players is owned by iPod. So, from 2002 to 2004 it is the Star of High Market share and High market growth (filled in grey in the figure below). Though the sales were not extraordinary in this period, they were a monopoly, and had practically no competition.

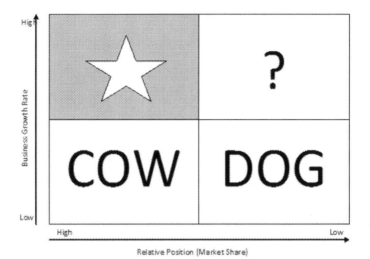

Figure 4.6: The position as on 2004.

In 2004, the growth was reduced and market share kept increasing with less reinvestment, and the cash generated was used to other products like iPhone which also eventually became a cash cow.

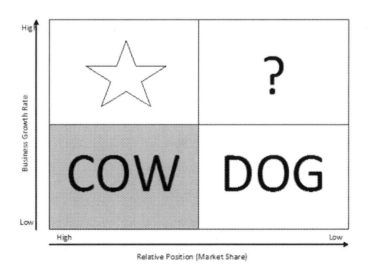

Figure 4.7: The position after 2004.

After being in the star matrix, it cannot sustain long in Star because of huge investments needed to sustain. The position should either go towards dog or cow and luckily iPod went to the cash cow region generating huge amount of cash.

7. PRODUCT INNOVATION MODEL FOR iPod

Being a product of entertainment the iPod was welcome by everyone easily. The fact that iPod did not have strong competitors made customers to throng the Apple stores. The rate of adoption in case of iPod has been really high. In a span of 5 years the iPod was able to reach even the traditional Laggards which might be a record. These 5 years can be divided into 2 phases. Until 2004 when it was compatible only with Mac machines only the innovators, early adopters and a part of early majority bought the product which is represented in grey below:

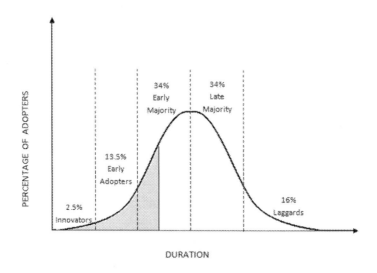

Figure 4.8: The position in 2004.

As the model suggests, the innovators and early adopters were targeted and then others followed. After the compatibility problems were resolved and with USB connection in 2004, the rest of the categories of people joined the customer market which is shown in grey below:

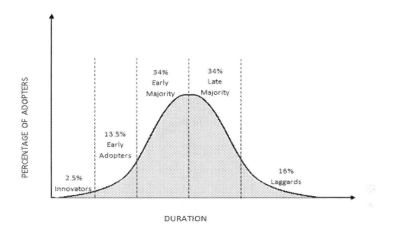

Figure 4.9: The position after 2004.

8. **CUSTOMER SATISFACTION MODEL FOR iPod**

From 2004 to 2008, the iPod has moved from a Performance product to an Excitement product especially after the introduction of mini iPod and cheaper iPods, it was more than what customers expected. That particular region is filled with black here. As, one can see, it has never been in the negative side of the axis.

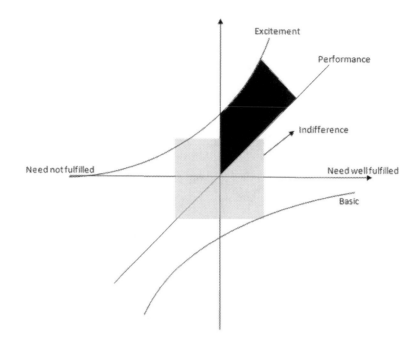

Figure 4.10: Customer Satisfaction Model from 2004 to 2008

9. CONCLUSION

The Apple's iPod is grown to such a stage that it has created a new accessories industry which produces case and speaker systems for iPods and is estimated to be a $300 million business (Reppel et. al., 2006). That speaks a lot about the product iPod and its impact. It is in fact become part of the US culture. The marketing models which were dealt can be used for strategic changes only when the models are analysed by people with objective insight (Mayo, 2006). In future, rather than pulling consumers from competitors, Apple should target the consumers who have not moved to the digital world yet, the group which still lives in the non-digital world which could be a potential market rather than concentrating on the competitors. This can be achieved by cheaper designs and easy to use facilities.

REFERENCES

Jacowski, Tony (2007). "The Kano Model And Six Sigma" *The Kano Model And Six Sigma EzineArticles.com*.[Online] http://ezinearticles. com/?The-Kano-Model-And-Six-Sigma&id=892407 [Accessed 27th May 2008]

Lloyd D. (2004). *"Instant Expert: A Brief History of iPod"* [Online] http://www.ilounge.com/index.php/articles/comments/instant-expert-a-brief-history-of-ipod/ [Accessed 28th May 2008]

Mayo, Donna T. (2006). *"Strategic Planning Tools"* [Online] http://www. referenceforbusiness.com/management/Sc-Str/Strategic-Planning-Tools.html [Accessed 28th May 2008]

Nutton, S. E. (2007). "Management Accounting - Business Strategy." *Financial Management*. pg. 43, 3 pgs [Available for Athens users at] http://proquest.umi.com/pqdweb?index=2&did=1197137941&Srch Mode=1&sid=1&Fmt=4&VInst=PROD&VType=PQD&RQT=309 &VName=PQD&TS=1212006777&clientId=28275 [Accessed 28th May 2008]

Reppel, A. E., Szmigin, I., Gruber, T. (2006). "The iPod phenomenon: identifying a market leader's secrets through qualitative marketing research." *Journal of Product & Brand Management*. 15(4), Pg 239-249. [Available for Athens users at] http://www.emeraldinsight.com/Insight/ ViewContentServlet?Filename=Published/EmeraldFullTextArticle/ Articles/0960150402.html [Accessed 28th May 2008]

Shockman C. (2000). *"Innovation Adoption for Third Party Property Management Companies"* [Online] http://www.osti.gov/bridge/servlets/ purl/776623-OFcsZg/webviewable/776623.pdf [Accessed 27th May 2008]

Sireli, Y., Kauffmann, P., Ozan, E. (2005). "Kano's model for multiple product development." *Journal of the Academy of Business and Economics*. March ed. [Online] http://findarticles.com/p/articles/mi_m0OGT/ is_3_5/ai_n16619670/pg_1 [Accessed 28th May 2008]

Smith, S. M., Swinyard, W. R. (1999). *"Chapter 6 - Product Planning Models"* [Online] http://marketing.byu.edu/htmlpages/courses/693r/modelsbook/chapter6.html [Accessed 28th May 2008]

Walton, G. (2007). "Theory, research and practice in library management 2: the balanced product portfolio." *Library Management.* 28(4/5), Pg 262-268 [Available for Athens users at] http://www.emeraldinsight.com/Insight/ViewContentServlet?Filename=Published/EmeraldFullTextArticle/Articles/0150280410.html [Accessed 28th May 2008]

CHAPTER – V

MARKETING ORIENTATION AND PLANNING

1. INTRODUCTION

To understand the marketing principles and management, we need to address questions like how marketing affects customer value, how strategic planning is carried out at different levels of the organization, what a marketing plan includes and how management can assess marketing performance.

We intend to answer these questions in the context of profit and non-profit organizations taking into account the shrinking world. Though the world is now called a global village, every person is unique in their own way and marketing has to find ways in which a standardized product is sold to non-standardized group of customers.

The different ways of market orientation and the market planning are dealt. The chosen marketing methods are:

Context	Marketing Principle	Company
Market Orientation	Benchmarking	Indian Bank Industry
Market Orientation	Good Mission Statements	Johnson & Johnson
Market Planning	Market Planning	National Health Services
Globalization	Five Core Business Processes	McDonald
Globalization	SWOT Analysis	Huwaei (Chinese Co.)

2. BENCHMARKING

An extensive study on "Performance benchmarking and strategic homogeneity of Indian banks" has been done (Mukherjee *et al.*, 2000). The authors designed their benchmarking based on two questions about how a performance benchmarking of the Indian banking sector can be obtained from their financial parameters and whether any groupings of the Indian banks can be obtained based on homogeneity in business strategies.

They used the following input and output parameters to measure the performance of banks.

Input variables	Output variables
Net Worth	Deposit
Borrowings	Net Profit
Operating Expenses	Advances
Number of Employees	Non-interest income
Number of Branches	Interest Spread

a. **Organizational costs and performance measures**

The banks are appraised as how individuals are appraised; in terms of self appraisal and peer appraisal to discuss the efficiency of the bank. In the self appraisal, the DEA approach is used. DEA is a linear programming technique used for measuring relative efficiency for a set of homogeneous decision-making units (DMUs) in converting multiple inputs (resources) to produce multiple outputs (performances). According to the DEA approach in the "best practice" units the efficiency is calculated to be one. It is based on set of inputs and outputs for each of the entity in two ways. One, given the set of inputs, the much or more output units has to be produced. And second, given the set of outputs, very little or less inputs should be used. If the decision-making units are not efficient enough, the efficiency tends to be less than one. The uniqueness of this DEA approach is that when creating a linear equation, the company can establish their own weights for inputs and outputs which might hide their weaknesses in order to improve the efficiency figure and to show themselves self-efficient. This is avoided by doing cross efficiency which is a relative efficiency measurement (Mukherji *et. al*, 2002).

b. **Competitor costs and performance measures**

After giving weights for the efficiency by the management of banks, the weights are compared to the competitors' weights. Every company would have rated itself good so that efficiency is improved, but when comparing the weights with their competitors for the same output, their relative position can be determined in the industry. This is carried out for all the banks. So virtually, the weights chosen by each bank for its own benefit is used to find the efficiency of each of its peers and the process is called "peer-efficiency" measurement (Mukherji *et. al,* 2002).

They also came up with the third stage of identification of clustering of strategically homogeneous banks. They separated the good performers coming together to form their own group with the bad performers getting segregated into other groups. Within each group, the best performers were chosen using their cross-efficiency measures and the set of best performers from each group constituted the paragon set which can be taken as the representative of the entire set of banks considered in this study. The members of this paragon set are inherently similar in strategy but better in performance than the other banks in the same cluster. So, the first objective of all the banks in each cluster would be to try to follow the measures adopted by their paragon set member in order to improve their own performance (Mukherji *et. al,* 2002).

This method of benchmarking is a reactive kind of market orientation, with this you can become the best in the industry, but it does not directly make you go beyond. To go beyond, the company should be more stable and proactive in marketing orientations and in coming up with innovations (Mukherji *et. al,* 2002).

3. GOOD MISSION STATEMENTS

An organization develops a mission statement to share with managers, employees, and-in many cases-customers. A clear, thoughtful mission statement provides employees with a shared sense of purpose, direction, and opportunity and guides geographically dispersed employees to work independently and collectively toward realizing the organization's goals. The case we are going to take is that of Johnson & Johnson (J&J). The reason for choosing this company is that the average tenure of employees in J&J is an eye-popping 15 years, quite an achievement in times when job-hopping is the norm. And the credit for this, goes to the company's Credo, a document which defines the way it functions, its responsibilities to, first, the consumer, then its employees, then the environment and society and finally, its shareholders. This isn't just a value statement, which even bogus companies can have, but a working document based on trust, respect and fairness (Lath, 2006).

a. Focus on limited number of goals

The mission statement of J&J defines limited number of goals to achieve and the goals are prioritised in the following order: Customers, Employees, Community, Stock holders.

b. Stress major policies and values

The values are mentioned in such a way that every person involved in the business gets a fair share. The customers should get high quality and reasonable cost, suppliers and distributors should get a fair profit, the employees' dignity is respected and their merits are recognized, protecting the environment and natural resources and stockholders should realize a fair return.

c. Define major competitive sphere

With regards to competitive advantages for employees, the mission statement states about compensation, working conditions and help employees fulfill their family responsibilities. It also talks about the ways in which employees can feel free to make suggestions and complaints. The equal opportunity based on qualification is touched upon and management is promised to be just and ethical.

Though the mission statement is meant to everyone connected to the business, it is employees who get inspired more, as it is part of their everyday work and it also helps them as something to look upon in case of crisis. It should inspire people when they are down and show new ways that are ahead during success.

4. MARKET PLANNING

Let's see the market reforms in NHS (non-profit organization) that took effect in 1990 in terms of general market planning.

a. Situation analysis (where are we now?)

From its inception in 1948 until the 1980s, the NHS enjoyed a solid reputation among its citizens and health-systems analysts for providing all residents with publicly funded, comprehensive health services, which were free at point of delivery. But during the 1980s the NHS experienced serious fiscal difficulties and became the target of sharp criticism (Harrison cites Klein, 1989).

b. Marketing Objectives (where do we want to go?)

The NHS wanted to make internal market reforms along the following lines (Harrison, 2004):

- To reduce the chronic shortages of beds and staff
- To enhance integration among care sectors
- To improve resource use
- Enhance and equalize the quality of care
- Set performance standards for hospitals

c. Marketing strategy (which way is best)

A market reform program was drafted which contained the following core elements (Harrison, 2004):

- Separation of public purchasers and providers of hospital services.

- Reorganization of hospitals, ambulance services, and providers of community social care as semi-autonomous trusts.

- Strengthening the role of GP (General Practitioner) in health care delivery and creating an arrangement whereby GPs could become fund holders, and acting as knowledgeable purchasers of health services for their patients

- Integrating health services sectors.

d. Financial projections/budgets (how can we be sure we got there?)

Being a non-profit organization, the NHS doesn't have to meet some financial constraints. But they have their own projections as to how to use the budget effectively (the government boosted real spending on NHS by 15.5%).

e. Implementation controls

To boost the performance of new reforms like competition among NHS hospitals and among primary care providers. This was supposed to unleash powerful incentives to use resources efficiently and improve quality of care. Besides boosting efficiency and quality, the reform was expected to insure greater representation and empowerment of patients within organizations responsible for using public funds to purchase, or commission, care (Harrison, 2004).

The torrent of additional funding during the formative years of the reform supported development of fund holding practices, rising managerial costs, and acquisition of management information systems by the NHS bureaucracy and trusts (Harrison, 2004).

Second, top government policy makers shifted from initial benefits of a free market for health care towards a policy of 'managed competition' – which acknowledged that the government must actively regulate purchasers, providers, and the negotiations among them.

Third, the government renewed and intensified its campaign from the 1980s for top-down control over health providers. This growing centralization of NHS operations clashed with the government's initial policy of devolving authority and budgets and allowing market forces to determine the distribution, quality and costs, and services.

Fourth, the government gradually intensified and extended its support for a 'primary-care led NHS', in which 'decisions about health care are taken as close to patients as possible, with a greater voice for patients and their carers in such decisions (NHS Executive, 1996).'

Fifth, during the 1990s the government placed additional stress on improving health outcomes, as well as boosting operating efficiency (Harrison, 2004).

The major problems NHS faced in implementing the strategies are the friction between the perceptions of business managers and that of the physicians. They are the best in their own respects and have their own level of ego and priorities when decisions have to be taken. This incompatibility is reduced by giving the physicians and managers cross training to some extent and explaining the difference in the contexts to both of them, so that at least people whether business managers or doctors can understand what others have to say.

5. FIVE CORE BUSINESS PROCESSES

Today we live in a global village because of the impact of mass communication and modern technology on society. In the business context, various factors can lead companies and organizations to market their products internationally. The decision to engage in international marketing may be driven by a single factor or a combination of several factors. There is also a difference between globalisation and internationalisation. Globalisation is about identifying the factors common across borders and internationalisation is to customize depending on the local environment (Groucutt *et al*, 2004). Let's take the example of McDonald's which is present in 116 countries and its basic marketing strategy is to think global and act local (Vignali, 2001).

a. Market sensing

McDonald realized a market outside USA early on and ventured in Canada in 1967. McDonald started using the franchising method in Canada and built a network of 640 restaurants, which made Canada the most lucrative market outside the USA. Because of franchising, the US brand culture was delivered and interpreted by local population in terms of product and service (Vignali, 2001).

b. Customer relationship management

One of the keys for McDonald's success is that they adapted to the local customer relationship management methods. For instance, in US usually technology replaces human workers, but Beijing is a different place altogether. So, they deployed people to interact personally to the customers. A public relations unit with 2 officers was set up in every outlet and everyday and they are available for customer's questions. Also 5 to 10 female receptionists are assigned to take care of kids and also talk to their parents. This kind of courtesy is unique and a big thing in Far East and so has to be taken into account by McDonald.

This does not hold true in UK, where people don't mind eating just their meal and leave the restaurant (Vignali, 2001).

The different pricing of McDonald's Big Mac in various countries is shown in APPENDIX - II (Vignali, 2001).

This is internationalisation, but McDonald does globalisation as well. They announced a global alliance with Walt Disney in 1997 which allowed them to share marketing rights for everything from films to food, for the next 10 years. So, McDonald added toys in their "happy meals" for animated films such as "A Bug's Life", "Toy Story", and the latest Tarzan. This was possible because Walt Disney has an appeal world-wide which spans across different communities.

McDonald also took some social responsibility though the Millennium Dreamers Global Children's recognition program along with Walt Disney and UNESCO. This is a program for young people to voice their views and take action for a better world.

c. **New offering realization**

The growth potential in the international market was realized by McDonald and irrespective of the demand and response they open 300-400 outlets every year. They in fact regret that they could have done this before when the competition was a lot thinner. This also means that a lot of the competitors' restaurants could have been theirs. So, they don't want the same thing to repeat and they grow rapidly in the other countries especially those where the competition is weak and can easily be entered. For example in Japan, they added 415 restaurants which accounted to be 25% of total expansions in 1998. Countries like Mexico, China and Italy are considered to be long term markets and also potential market for opening new markets.

At the same time, it is also true that the base USA market has saturated and in fact McDonald has no much of a choice than to expand geographically to keep the pace on. The Asian and South American markets are considered to be increasing in the coming years. This is represented in the graph below (Vignali, 2001 cites Kotler, 1994).

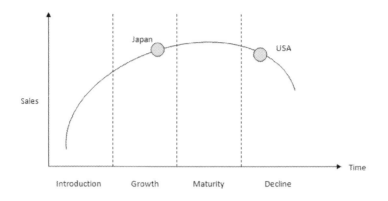

Figure 5.1: The graph for the position of McDonald's in Japan and USA as on 1994

d. Fulfillment management

Standardization, to make the burger to taste the same whether in USA, Singapore or Spain, saves a lot of cost. But McDonald realized that adaptation to the local environment is really important for success. Therefore it stuck to the concept of "think global, act local.'

The consumers at different part of the world have their own tastes, preferences, laws and customs. And McDonald never failed to incorporate these, for example Israel has a practice of separating meat and cheese; which was accepted and implemented in the kosher restaurants. Hindus in India do not eat beef and Muslims do not eat pork and Jains (among others) do not eat any kind of meat. So vegetable nuggets were introduced and mutton based Maharaja Mac was introduced according to the local culture. In Singapore and Malaysia, the religious clerics inspected the McDonald's rigorously and gave a clean certificate (Vignali, 2001).

e. Customer acquisition

The Customer acquisition is done mainly by advertising, and McDonald's has a variety of campaigns according to the local culture of various countries. For example, in the UK, England footballer Alan Shearer was deployed to promote the hamburgers. In France, the international goalkeeper, Fabien Barthez is used. The point they are trying to put across to the public is the same across countries. But different personalities are chosen to put it across firmly.

In East Asia, McDonald's could not have had the success they have without their appeal to younger generations of consumer: children and teenagers. The corporation makes a point of cultivating this market and invests heavily in television advertising aimed specifically at children.

The McDonald did not rely on TV Advertisement in China, because in Chinese television programs, the ads are telecasted only at the end of the TV programs, so people don't really watch ads and tend to switch to other channels. So, McDonald relied a lot on print media. They also came up with a creative idea of pairing the company's male mascot with a female companion known as Aunt McDonald whose job is to entertain kids. This idea which worked in China might not work well in global market because in the West, the people might think that it is a cheap gimmick. But frankly, marketing and its effects cannot be always identified before implementing.

In contrast, in Hong Kong, McDonald's has made great efforts to present itself as a champion of environmental awareness and public welfare, as they see this as an important attribute to the local consumer. A leaflet comparing the Hong Kong fast food industry saw McDonald's adverts as: Promoting McDonald's as a local institution, with a clear stake in the overall health of the community (Vignali, 2001).

6. SWOT ANALYSIS

An effective marketing strategy can be drafted using the following model (Wee Tan, Ahmed, 1999 cite Sammon *et al* 1987*)* which includes environment trends, competitor analysis, market dynamics, inputs from secondary sources, market intelligence, entrepreneurial insights, strategic planning and implementation, opportunistic decisions and responses and lead to an "Effective Strategy."

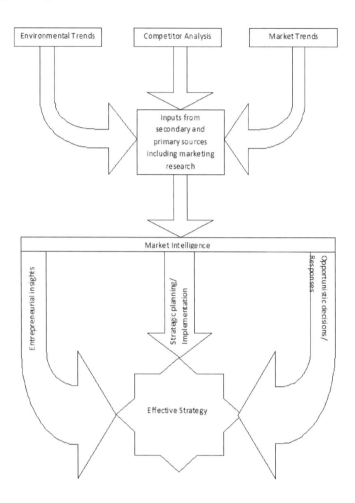

Figure 5.2: Components of an effective strategy

Let's build the marketing strategy for Huawei by doing SWOT Analysis using the above model as a reference. Huwaei is a China based company and is a leader in China in providing next generation telecommunications networks. It is slowly penetrating into the global arena, so it is wise to analyze in order to do a reality check about the position of the company based on the information given by Emerald (2007).

a. **Strengths**

- Highly skilled, vast and cheap workforce is something Chinese companies have at their disposal.

- Local market is vast, the highest population in the world and is the market every company in the world want a piece of.

- Competitive pricing and added value products.

- Almost half of the firm's employees are working in R&D, including some extremely learned and cutting-edge technicians.

- Using network convergence as a basis, it uses what are known as "Common Build Blocks" to enable customization of services.

- Alliances with NEC, Microsoft, Nokia, Siemens and Marconi.

- Huawei has four software research institutes, including one in India.

b. **Weaknesses**

- The sales is creeping around 5 billion dollars when compared to the global competitors.

- The company reduced its R&D budget from 13.5% to 10% in just two years from 2000 to 2002.

- A confusing state of being because of lack of adequate support from Chinese government.

- Chinese government's bureaucracy problems.

c. **Opportunities**

- The untapped markets of Third World Nations.

- Take advantage of the exchange rates of currencies by moving to the West.

- Learn the local demand and market nature of other Asian countries.

- Seek the direct help of the Chinese government.

d. **Threats**

- With regards to 3G technologies, there are 2 standards and China has not yet decided which one to embrace.

- Fears of Piracy

- High-ranking technicians' turn over.

- There are a lot of social, political economical problems in Africa which is cut off from the potential markets.

e. **Strategies**

- Give a clear picture of the international markets to the Chinese government in order to adopt the necessary standards and use for the local people.

- Reduce cost to match with pirated products or enhance quality so that there is a visible difference of added value in their products.

- Test the African market by investing a small fraction, specifically in countries which are politically in a better state.

- Expand to the Asian markets, where population density is high, by localising the product depending on the local demand.

- Expand to the West by cheaper prices.

6. CONCLUSION

As domestic market is getting saturated as time passes, brands seem to think beyond boundaries and it is not an easy path and has its own risks. But we can also see from the study that the standardised brand does not help totally. And it needs localisation to survive and succeed. Also from the study we were able to find that marketing is not some isolated department in a company. Every department of the company has to rely on the information and strategies of other departments and hence knowledge of everything is primarily important for a business aspirant.

REFERENCES

Bennett R. (1995) *International Marketing – Strategy, Planning, Market Entry & Implementation.* London: Kogan Page.

Emerald. (2007). Huawei at the crossroads - The dilemma at the heart of the next big telecoms giant. *Strategic Direction.* 23(8), 19-21 *[Available for Athens users at]* http://www.emeraldinsight.com/Insight/ViewContentServlet?Filename=Published/EmeraldFullTextArticle/Articles/0560230806.html

Groucutt J., Leadley P., Forsyth P. (2004). *Marketing – essential principles, new realities.* London, Sterling, VA: Kogan Page

Harrison M.I. (2004) *Implementing Change in Health Systems – Market Reforms in United Kingdom, Sweden & The Netherlands.* London, Thousand Oaks, CA, New Delhi: Sage.

Kotler P., Keller K.L. (2007) *A Framework for Marketing Management,* 3rd ed. New Jersey: Pearson.

Lath S. (2006). Johnson & Johnson: Living By Its Credo; J&J's mission statement places the interests of its employees above those of its shareholders. No wonder people don't want to leave. *Business Today.* New Delhi: Nov 5, 2006. pg. 126 *[Available for Athens users at]* http://proquest.umi.com/pqdweb?index=0&did=1157851991&SrchMode=1&sid=1&Fmt=3&VInst=PROD&VType=PQD&RQT=309&VName=PQD&TS=1205515740&clientId=28275

Mukherjee A., Nath P., Pal M.N. (2002). Performance benchmarking and strategic homogeneity of Indian banks. *International Journal of Bank Marketing.* 20(3), 122-139 *[Available for Athens users at]* http://www.emeraldinsight.com/Insight/ViewContentServlet?Filename=Published/EmeraldFullTextArticle/Articles/0320200303.html

Vignali, C. (2001). McDonald's: "think global, act local" – the marketing mix. *British Food Journal.* 103(2), 97-111 *[Available for Athens users at]*

http://www.emeraldinsight.com/Insight/ViewContentServlet?Filenam e=Published/EmeraldFullTextArticle/Articles/0701030201.html

Wee Tan, T. T. Ahmed Z. U. (1999). Managing market intelligence: an Asian marketing research perspective. *Marketing Intelligence & Planning.* 17(6) 298-306 *[Available for Athens users at]* http://www.emeraldinsight.com/Insight/ViewContentServlet?Filenam e=Published/EmeraldFullTextArticle/Articles/0200170605.html

ORGANISATIONAL STRATEGY

CHAPTER- VI

NIKE – GIVE IT A SWOOSH

1.0 INTRODUCTION

NIKE, Inc. is better known to the general public as the company which has a bratty but effective logo "Just do it." Founded in 1964 through an investment of $500 each by Phil Knight and Bill Bowerman, the company (then called Blue Ribbon Sports--BLS) has evolved from being an importer and distributor of Japanese specialty running shoes to becoming the world leader in the design, distribution and marketing of athletic footwear. What is so unique and interesting about this company? According to the CEO Phil Knight the current business model is the same as what it was when this whole thing started (Locke, 2002). That speaks volumes about this successful company and encourages business aspirants to research on the strategies adopted by the management team to preserve their genuineness. Let's delve into the path travelled by Nike from 1997 to 2007.

1.1 FOOTWEAR INDUSTRY

The whole US footwear industry had started to manufacture its goods in the low wage Asian countries. In course of time the stock turnover time had to be reduced, so operations demanded short lead times, so Mexico and certain Caribbean nations took over (Buxey, 2005).

1.2 SHORT HISTORY OF NIKE

Nike's business model was developed by Knight while attending Stanford Business School in the early 1960s. Knight realized that while lower-cost, high-quality Japanese producers were beginning to take over the US consumer appliance and electronics markets, most leading footwear companies (e.g., Adidas) were still manufacturing their own shoes in higher-cost countries like the United States and Germany. By outsourcing shoe production to lower-cost Japanese producers, Knight believed that Blue Ribbon Sports could undersell its competitors and break into this market. As a result, Blue Ribbon Sports began to import high-tech sports shoes from Onitsuka Tiger of Japan. As sales increased to almost $2 million in the early 1970s, BLS parted ways with Onitsuka and began to design and subcontract its own line of shoes. The Nike brand was launched in 1972, and the company officially changed its name to Nike, Inc. in 1978 (Locke, 2002).

1.3 OUTSOURCING

Today, Nike's products are manufactured in more than 700 factories, employing over 500,000 workers in 51 countries. Nike has only 22,658 direct employees, the vast majority working in the United States. The path travelled by Nike is not a bed of roses. Operating in 51 different countries is not easy at all, and Nike had to deal with the Perils of Globalization: Wages, Working Conditions and the Rise of the Anti-Nike Movement. For example, Low Wages in Indonesia, Child Labour in Pakistan, Health and Safety Problems in Vietnam, combined to tarnish Nike's image. As Phil Knight lamented in a May 1998 speech to the National Press Club, "the Nike product has become synonymous with slave wages, forced overtime, and arbitrary abuse" (Locke, 2002).

Nike's management team initially shrugged off the complaints and criticisms saying that it was not under their control, which is true in a way. But later took the issues seriously and replied back with strict rules and regulations. The minimum wage was increased to more than the country's minimum wage in Indonesia. It has also increased the minimum age of footwear factory workers to 18 and all other workers (in apparel, equipment) to 16 and insisted that all footwear suppliers adopt US Occupational Safety and Health Administration (OSHA) standards for indoor air quality. In fact, a quick review of some of Nike's recent efforts in the area of labour and environmental/health standards shows that the company is serious about doing the right thing. In the process of "Learning to Become a Global Corporate Citizen," Nike deployed New Staff with relevant global laws and code of conduct trainings, Increased Monitoring of Its Suppliers, and built Relations with International and Non-Profit Organizations (Locke, 2002).

Being a citizen of a developing nation, the author believes without this job these young kids have no choice but end up in begging and human trafficking for illegal businesses. This job at least will give some kind of a reason to live. It is not the problem of Nike, but in fact the problems of the government who ignore such humanistic and educational issues and indulge in selfish motives. The dawn for these kinds of labour issues has to come from a world revolution.

1.4 LEADERSHIP: Nike, Goddess of victory is led by the leader Phil Knight. Phil Knight is an ultra-competitive, clever, shrewd man who figured out a way to make all other athletic shoe companies irrelevant by connecting his products with the awe and romance of primordial athletic competition (Theodhosi, 2000). His profile of starting and running the Nike is shown below (Ma 1999 cites Klein, 1990 and Katz, 1994):

Inspiration: Cheaper Japanese-made cameras were able to compete with high-quality and more expensive German cameras.

Lesson: Germany – home of the industry leader, Adidas – was simply not the best place in the world to put shoe machines due to its higher labour cost.

Mission: Crush Adidas.

Strategy: high quality, low cost, and brand image.

Strategist: vision, ambition, passion, and keen knowledge of sports.

Implementation: dedicated and knowledgeable management team, flexible corporate structure, creative organizational culture, and competitive spirit.

Results: victory, winning, and persistent superior performance.

Phil Knight resigned from president and chief executive of Nike but remains chairman of the world's largest athletic shoe and clothing maker at a time when sales for the "swoosh" logo was growing around the globe.

1.5 STRATEGY

Nike came up with a three pronged strategy (Ma, 1999):

1. Strong R&D insures better quality and design.

2. Shifting manufacturing progressively to lower wage countries helps control manufacturing cost to the lowest possible, leaving higher margins for manoeuvring in marketing.

3. Effective advertising campaign, carefully orchestrated promotion effort, and celebrity endorsement facilitate the building and strengthening of the Nike image.

Their success is attributed to the fact that they never took any of these factors light. They reduced cost by manufacturing in lower wage countries, at the same time they did not compromise on the quality of design or product, or in fact even promotion. Though the company was in midst of controversies about problems regarding business ethics, they took it in their stride eventually and reacted with strong positive responses with corporate social responsibilities. The leadership needs mention, Phil Knight never tried to show a rosy picture regarding the controversies, he acted true to his conscience. His simple business model together with aggressive leadership qualities led Nike to the place they are now. The success is not a matter of chance, but it was meticulously planned and Nike achieved the position it is now by determined foresight of the leader.

1.6 COMPETITION

The U.S. footwear industry consists of about 100 manufacturers, 1500 wholesalers, and 30,000 retail outlets with combined annual retail revenue of $25 billion. The major shoe companies including Nike, Reebok, Adidas, Brown Shoe and Timberland, are mainly owners of brand names that "source" their shoes from independent manufacturers. The retail segment includes owners of large chains like Footlocker and thousands of small local retailers. The retail segment is highly concentrated: the largest 50 chains hold about 80% of market.

Many shoe companies work both in wholesale and retail segments (First Research, 2008).

Demand is driven by fashion and demographics. The profitability of individual companies depends on their ability to design and market attractive shoe models. Big companies have economies of scale in distribution and marketing. Small companies can compete successfully through superior design or marketing. (First Research, 2008).

1.6 LIFE CYCLE OF THE INDUSTRY

The footwear industry will exist as long as human have feet and use the feet to move around. So, the industry is not in a declining state in the near future. If we take Nike it has grown and declined on par with the industry sustaining the no.1 position.

The chosen life cycle model is that of Wasson (1974) which has the stages market development, rapid growth, competitive turbulence, saturation/maturity, and decline. Let's see the graph for Nike according to these stages.

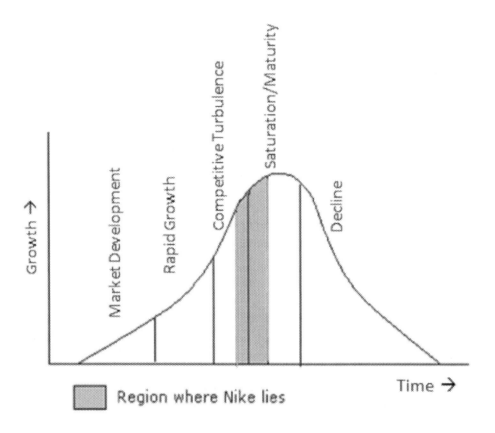

Figure 6.1: The life cycle of the footwear industry

1.7 The PESTLE Analysis for Nike for the period of 1997 to 2007

External Factors	No	Affecting the Organization	Implications in the Organization	Type of factor	Importance of Factor
Political	1.	War in Iraq	War in Iraq tarnished the brand image of U.S. In parts of the world, Osama bin laden was more famous than the popular American brands like Nike, McDonalds, and Coca-Cola.	Negative	Critical
	2.	Stand against counterfeiters	The Chinese government launched a major in Nov 2005 in a new offensive against manufacturers and retailers of counterfeit golf equipment in China.	Positive	Significant
Economic	1.	Depreciation of U.S. dollar	The decline of U.S. dollar against Asian countries' currencies would affect the outsourcing business.	Negative	Critical
	2.	Cost of fuel	The cost per barrel of crude oil has increased is a cause of concern.	Negative	Very Important
	3.	Inflation	The inflation of the US will play a role	Negative	Important
Social	1.	Shoes Logo controversy	In 1997, the logo used in some of the Nike brands shows a symbol which resembles the Arabic word for Allah which created controversy and the Muslim community demanded an apology, which was later, resolved.	Negative	Significant
	2.	Sweatshops	Anti sweatshops campaign in America was wide spread and gained momentum among the general public.	Negative	Very Important

Technological	1.	Introduction of RFID	Radio Frequency Identification (RFID) was found to be useful at a fundamental level to improve a firm's business processes and logistics.	Positive	Important
Legal	1.	Labour problems	The labour problems in Indonesia, Pakistan and Vietnam created legal threats which were resolved	Negative	Very Important
	2.	Nike v. Kasky Case	Regarding the labour policies of Nike an individual filed a case and the Supreme Court issued an unsigned order that stated it should never have taken the case.	Positive	Important
Environmental	1.	Eco friendly products	Nike launched the first performance basketball shoe made from manufacturing waste.	Positive	Significant
	2.	Alternative to chemically treated clothing	Nike used fine natural fabrics made from organic cotton, wool and linen, tencel (made from wood pulp), hemp, bamboo, Ingeo (made from corn) and silk that are used to create sharp, stylish outfits.	Positive	Significant

1.8 PORTER'S FIVE FORCES ANALYSIS FOR NIKE

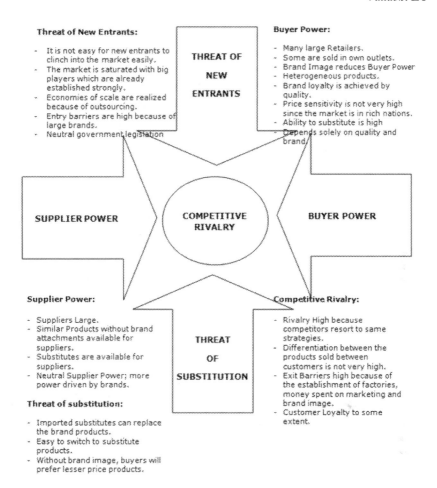

Threat of New Entrants:

- It is not easy for new entrants to clinch into the market easily.
- The market is saturated with big players which are already established strongly.
- Economies of scale are realized because of outsourcing.
- Entry barriers are high because of large brands.
- Neutral government legislation

Buyer Power:

- Many large Retailers.
- Some are sold in own outlets.
- Brand Image reduces Buyer Power
- Heterogeneous products.
- Brand loyalty is achieved by quality.
- Price sensitivity is not very high since the market is in rich nations.
- Ability to substitute is high
- Depends solely on quality and brand.

Supplier Power:

- Suppliers Large.
- Similar Products without brand attachments available for suppliers.
- Substitutes are available for suppliers.
- Neutral Supplier Power; more power driven by brands.

Threat of substitution:

- Imported substitutes can replace the brand products.
- Easy to switch to substitute products.
- Without brand image, buyers will prefer lesser price products.

Competitive Rivalry:

- Rivalry High because competitors resort to same strategies.
- Differentiation between the products sold between customers is not very high.
- Exit Barriers high because of the establishment of factories, money spent on marketing and brand image.
- Customer Loyalty to some extent.

Figure 6.2: Porter's five forces for Nike

2.0 THE NEW NIKE

From few years before 2004, the company has devoted as much energy to the mundane details of running a business such as developing top-flight information systems, logistics, and supply-chain management as it does to marketing coups and cutting-edge sneaker design. More and more, Nike was searching for the right balance between its creative and its business sides, relying on a newfound financial and managerial discipline to drive growth. This is covered extensively in Business Week September issue of 2004.

2.1 THE STRATEGY

In the old days, Nike operated pretty much on instinct. It took a guess as to how many pairs of shoes to churn out and hoped it could cram them all onto retailers' shelves. Not anymore. Nike has overhauled its computer systems to get the right number of sneakers to more places in the world more quickly. By methodically studying new markets, it has become a powerhouse overseas -- and in new market segments that it once scorned, such as soccer and fashion. It has also beefed up its management team. And after stumbling with its acquisitions, Nike has learned to manage those brands -- Cole Haan dress shoes, Converse retro-style sneakers, Hurley International skateboard gear, and Bauer in-line and hockey skates -- more efficiently. Indeed, part of Nike's growth strategy is to add to its portfolio of brands.

Knight made his boldest management move in 2001, when he named two long time Nike insiders, creative brand and design wonk Mark G. Parker and operations maven Charles D. Denson, as co-presidents. With Grossman and Blair providing an outsider's perspective and with Parker and Denson steeped in the company's culture, Knight hoped to achieve a balance between the old and the new, the creative and the financially responsible.

In the old days at Nike, the culture encouraged local managers to spend big and to go flat-out for market share instead of profitability. This led to an undisclosed loss in Paris Soccer Park for the 1998 World Cup. So Parker and Denson engineered a matrix structure that breaks down managerial responsibility both by region and product. Because the company pumps out 120,000 products every year in four different launch cycles, local managers always had plenty of choice -- but also plenty of ways to mess up. Under the matrix, Nike headquarters establishes which products to push and how to do it, but regional managers are allowed some leeway to modify those edicts. The matrix won't guarantee that another fiasco like the Paris soccer park cannot occur, but it makes it a lot less likely.

Nike aims to keep pace in the techno-battle with Nike Free, a shoe still being tested, that makes runners feel as if they were barefoot. It's inspired by the barefoot runners of Kenya, who have proved that shoeless training builds strength and improves performance. Nike made basketball shoes into an off-the-court fashion statement, its latest product "Total 90s" have become fashion accessories for folks who may never get closer to a soccer pitch than the stands.

If we want to analyse the strategy chosen by Nike, it is in fact both emergent and deliberate but Nike woke up to the alarm bell without losing much, at least on record. The strategy is simple, give an honest look to the status of the company without complacency or prejudice, to accept failures if any and take responsibilities and react positively to implement robust and well planned changes. Here again the leader by all definitions CEO Phil Knight rose up to the occasion, took exactly the right decisions during an almost cringe crisis situation. Those are situations when the leadership is most sought after and for leader it is the most difficult task ahead to handle the pressures from all directions from finance to marketing to HR and what not. And also the change in the organizational structure is very innovative, because they did not remove the power of totally which will demoralise the managers and also giving too much power will end up in wrong spending. This shows very well that companies are successful not because of sheer luck, but because of well executed innovative strategies taken before it is required and demanded.

2.2 TOWS ANALYSIS

The TOWS Analysis of the strategies chosen by Nike is shown below, the Strengths, Weaknesses, Opportunities and Threats before 2001 are listed and the strategies chosen are shown here. So, outer cells are the state of Nike in 2001 and before and the inner four cells are the strategies chosen in 2002 and later depending on the status of the company.

TOWS ANALYSIS	External Opportunities (O) 1. Increase the social responsibility. 2. R&D to develop improved models for sports people. 3. Come up with attractive models for general public which is similar to their sports icons. 4. Technical advancement in supply chain and manufacturing 5. Better organization structure. 6. Expand geographically.	External Threats (T) 1. Devaluation of dollar 2. Rising Cost in Low wage countries. 3. Asian competitors selling at low price. 4. Increased aggressive competition.
Internal Strengths (S) 1. Established Brand. 2. The cost of production is low. 3. The No. 1 in the market 4. Best Leadership in place 5. The markets are rich nations.	*Strategies that use strengths to maximize opportunities. (SO)* 1. Being no. 1 in the market helped them to invest on R&D and come up with innovative models. 2. The Brand was used to come up with socially responsible manufacturing. 3. Their brand name helped them expand geographically.	*Strategies that use strengths to minimize threats. (ST)* 1. Since the markets are rich nations, they are slightly price insensitive. 2. Because of Best leadership qualities of Phil Knight and the brand name the competition is kept under control.

Internal Weaknesses (W)	Strategies that minimize weaknesses by taking advantage of opportunities. (WO)	Strategies that minimize weaknesses and avoid threats.(WT)
1. Organizational structure is not under total control.	1. The organisation was restructured using better leadership qualities.	1. Reduce threats by concentrating on the successful products.
2. Too much money spent on Marketing with unpredictable returns.	2. Better technology was used to predict the market.	2. Shifting to countries where production cost is lower than the current costs.
3. Too many different products	3. Strict labour policies were put in place.	
4. The production details are based on gut feeling.	4. RFID was used in the Supply Chain management.	
5. Infamous labour policies controversies.		
6. Less Efficient Supply Chain		

2.3 BOWMAN'S STRATEGY CLOCK

The Nike's position before and after the strategy is shown below.

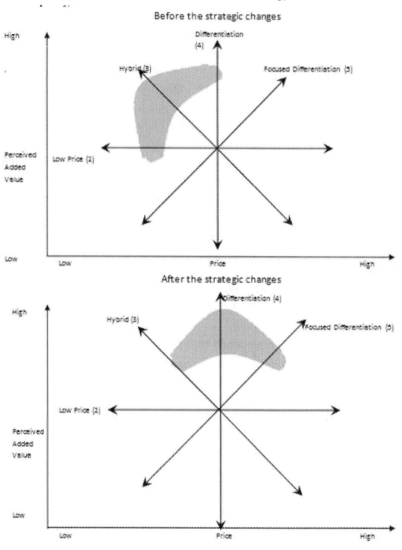

Figure 6.3: The position before and after the implementation of the strategy

2.4 ROLE OF STAKE HOLDERS

In the case of Nike, the most influential stake holders are the customers. Nike, originally the target of a sweeping sweatshop campaign because of the abysmal conditions in its overseas factories, is now leading the apparel industry in sector-wide reform to increase transparency and improve labour standards. Also, Nike started concepts like green accounting and environment friendly products to strengthen its brand because of the pressures from the stakeholders. The stakeholders here require more than just keeping them informed. They need to be satisfied, because the competitor's power cannot be underestimated. So, Nike's strategies are influenced by the stakeholders for the better. And Nike has to act in order to satisfy the stakeholders.

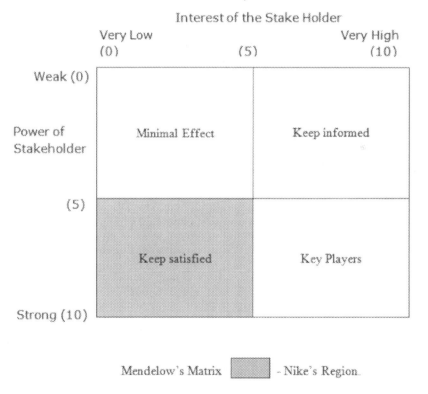

Figure 6.4: Mendelow's Matrix for stakeholders (Power/Interest Matrix)

2.5 NIKE

The future is now! The future of business in Nike does not lie in just increasing production. It in fact lies in whether they are successful in predicting, sustaining and controlling their market by heuristics and use that in the production. This lies in enhancing and exploiting their resources to increase the prediction and control capabilities in the ever changing market. Sounds impossible? Many things which were impossible in the past are part of everyday life now. It cannot happen overnight but failures and successes teach equal lessons. So, it is more of FIT than stretch.

ANSOFF'S MATRIX: The same idea is shown below in the Ansoff's matrix used by business strategists. Also, the TOWS for the future strategies are shown below.

Figure 6.5: Ansoff's Matrix for the future Nike

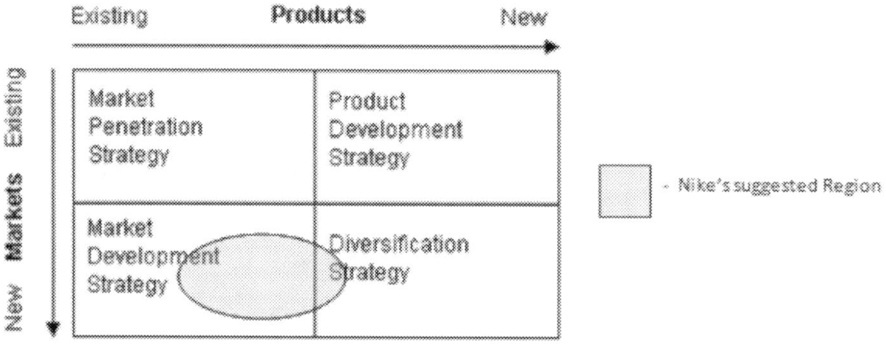

2.6 TOWS Analysis for future:

TOWS ANALYSIS FOR FUTURE	External Opportunities (O) 1. Increase the ability to Predict, sustain and control the market. 2. Increase the use of technology. 3. Experiment a little with marketing.	External Threats (T) 1. The change in focus might give way to the competitors to go ahead in the market share. 2. Concentrating less on marketing might cause problems.
Internal Strengths (S) 1. Established Brand. 2. The cost of production is low. 3. The No. 1 in the market 4. Best Leadership in place 5. The markets are rich nations.	*Strategies that use strengths to maximize opportunities.(SO)* 1. Nike is way ahead in the market so they should increase the use of technology to experiment a little with marketing.	*Strategies that use strengths to minimize threats.(ST)* 1. The established brand should be used to change slight focus in the marketing strategy.
Internal Weaknesses (W) 1. Too much money spent on Marketing with unpredictable returns. 2. Not able to determine the market expense to sustain.	*Strategies that minimize weaknesses by taking advantage of opportunities. (WO)* 1. The market is still not totally under control, so Nike should increase the use of technology and predict, sustain and control the market.	*Strategies that minimize weaknesses and avoid threats.(WT)* 1. The marketing heuristics should be enhanced and the shift in market focus should be done with a lot of planning and should take into account the possible competitor's tactics.

3.0 CONCLUSION

As the Nike commercial stated during the 1996 Olympic Games: You don't win Silver, you lose the Gold. "We are in this business to win," claimed Knight. And win they did (Ma, 1999).

REFERENCES:

Aaronson, Susan Ariel (2002), Broadening corporate responsibility: is maximizing shareholder value alone a good enough long-term strategy?, The International Economy [online] http://www.thefreelibrary.com/Broadening+corporate+responsibility:+is+maximizing+shareholder+value...-a092725516 [Accessed 22nd January 2008

Anonymous (1997), Footwear, Adweek, Dallas: (Southwest edition) Pg. 119, 1 pgs (Issue: Oct 20 1997) http://proquest.umi.com/pqdweb?index=46&did=22070543&SrchMode=1&sid=3&Fmt=4&VInst=PROD&VType=PQD&RQT=309&VName=PQD&TS=1203361605&clientId=28275 [Accessed 22nd January 2008]

Business Week Cover Story (2004), The New Nike [online] http://www.businessweek.com/magazine/content/04_38/b3900001_mz001.htm [Accessed 22nd January 2008]

Buxey, Geoff (2005), Globalisation and manufacturing strategy in the TCF industry, International Journal of Operations & Production Management, 25(2), 100-113 [online] http://www.emeraldinsight.com/Insight/ViewContentServlet?Filename=Published/EmeraldFullTextArticle/Articles/0240250201.html [Accessed 22nd January 2008]

First Research (2008), Footwear Manufacture, Wholesale, and Retail - Industry Profile [online] http://www.researchandmarkets.com/reportinfo.asp?report_id=302266 [Accessed 22nd January 2008]

Locke, Richard M. (2002), The Promise and Perils of Globalization: The Case of Nike [online] http://web.mit.edu/polisci/research/locke/nikepaperFINAL.pdf [Accessed 22nd January 2008]

Ifp (2007) ACCA F1 Accountant in Business Study Text [online] http://books.google.com/books?id=dc1_qRvu7W4C&dq=mendelow's+Power/Interest&source=gbs_summary_s&cad=0 [Accessed 23rd January 2008]

Ma, Hao (1999), Constellation of competitive advantage: components and dynamics, Management Decision, 37(4), 348-356 [online] http://

www.emeraldinsight.com/Insight/ViewContentServlet?Filename=Published/EmeraldFullTextArticle/Articles/0010370405.html [Accessed 22nd January 2008]

MAHONEY, ANN I. (2000), Living the brand, Association Management [online] http://www.thefreelibrary.com/Living+the+brand.-a062712876 [Accessed 22nd January 2008]

McCarry, Deanna (2002), Green accounting: a new route to corporate transparency? [online] http://findarticles.com/p/articles/mi_m0ICC/is_3_71/ai_91967437 [Accessed 22nd January 2008]

Theodhosi, Alexander S. (2000), May the worst man win, Strategy & Leadership, 28(3), 28-31 [online] http://www.emeraldinsight.com/Insight/ViewContentServlet?Filename=Published/EmeraldFullTextArticle/Articles/2610280305.html [Accessed 22nd January 2008]

MANAGING CHANGE

CHAPTER – VII

CORPORATE RECOVERY OF CONTINENTAL AIRLINES

இடுக்கண் வருங்கால் நகுக அதனை
அடுத்தூர்வது அஃதொப்பது இல்

- திருக்குறள் (621)

The above lines are one of the Thirukkural couplets of a Tamil (One of the South Indian Languages) poet and saint Thiruvalluvar. It means *"Laugh your trouble/sorrow away. There is no other way to conquer woes."* Though these lines are centuries old, it is a lot relevant even in today's business world during crisis. The first step to follow in any crisis situation is to immediately come out emotionally from the crisis and think as if it is happening to some other company and you have been asked to resolve it. This is also the reason why managers seek professional corporate recovery consultants to resolve the crisis in hand.

Slatter, 1984, defines, "Corporate Recovery is about the management of firms in crisis, firms that will become insolvent unless appropriate management actions are taken to effect a turnaround in their financial information..... [So,] Turnaround management therefore is not a freak occurrence; it is part of everyday business." But what is a turnaround situation? Certainly whenever there is a cash crisis there is a turnaround situation. But it may exist when there is no cash crisis as well. A broad definition of what constitutes a turnaround situation recognizes that, firms often exhibit symptoms of failure long before any crisis begins. Such firms are often stagnant businesses with underutilized assets and ineffective management.

Now let's see the causes of failure. Slatter, (1984) points out eleven frequently occurring factors which are the principal causes of corporate decline. They are Poor Management, Inadequate Financial Control, Competition, High Cost Structure, and Changes in Market Demand, Adverse Movements in Commodity Prices, Big Projects, Acquisitions, Financial Policy, and Overtrading. If you look at these causes closely you can see that all these are because of **COMPLACENCY** at some level or some section. But there could also be some external factors which are out of company's control. Elliott, (2007) describes the external factors as Political and legal causes, Economic causes, Socio-cultural causes, Technological causes.

This case study is about a company which belongs to airline industry, the industry which is usually described as a roller-coaster ride, it goes up and down, and it is either feast or famine. The chosen company is Continental Airlines which is one of the companies that underwent a turnaround situation caused by terrorist attack on the WTO on September 11 2001. Combs (2002) says, "September 11 was a severe blow to an industry already battered by the rapid decline in business-related travel following the collapse of the dot-com bubble". A worldwide economic slump was impacted because of 9/11, and was experienced over the next few years. Especially the airline industry was the worst affected being described as turbulent; tumultuous; political and legal nightmare.

Experts (Dark Skies, 2004) say that the major setback in the airline industry happened because of the following reasons:

Fallout in demand: The important reason for the set back in the airline industry is the lack of demand which is not unique to airline industry; any industry or market can attain such a saturation point in its life cycle. But here in the airlines industry, they lost the customers' confidence.

Over Capacity: The inappropriate growth of the airlines industry, where the airline capacity was increased expecting the fantastic growth to continue for not including resilience plan in case of emergency let them to chase few customers.

War and illness: The travel to Middle East was affected by the war in Iraq and the tourists to Asian destinations were affected by SARS. So, it turned out to be a double jeopardy for the airline industry. Almost one third of the passengers did not travel because of different forms of fear. And because of the war in Iraq, the fuel prices started to increase. The Financial Times reported saying as little as 1 cent increase in 1 gallon fuel will end up in an increase of almost $180 million overall cost for an airline.

Budget competition: To add to these pressures, new threats were sensed because of the low cost airlines like easyJet and Ryanair in Europe and Jetblue and SouthWest in USA. This was a wakeup call for many existing airlines.

Pre-existing troubles: The reasons for failure cannot be attributed totally to the external factors. Many airlines were already in a messed up state and were in a weak organizational structure to start with.

Jackson *et al* (2004) say that at Continental, a poor reputation in the industry and a new CEO were the forces that drove a major turnaround effect. Before its turnaround, Continental airline was on the verge of bankruptcy for the third time. That's when the company began a complete transformation that rivalled the Cinderella's at the stroke of midnight. CEO Gordon Bethune initiated the change effort by setting out the strategic goals and specific measure of success:

1. *Fly to win.* The goal was to achieve top quartile industry profit margins.

2. *Fund the Future.* To do so required reducing interest expense by owning more hub real estate.

3. *Make reliability a reality.* Specific goals included ranking among the top airlines on the four measurements used by U.S. department of Transportation.

4. *Work Together.* Have a company where employees enjoy working and are valued for their contributions.

Bethune believed that mutual admiration and cooperation at all level of the organization structure is an important way to the success. He also believed in teams rather than individuals. When an employee is honoured, the employee should accept the honour on behalf of the whole team and the success should be shared so as to make everybody sit up straight and feel good. So that, the next day the employees would work harder and smarter for the company's success. In the end, essentially it is to acknowledge and appreciate the contribution from others so that they develop a sense of belongingness.

D'Agostino, (2006) has done an extensive investigation on the take off of Continental Airlines from crisis. The company's established a strategy to "Identify and increase the loyalty of Continental's most valuable customers. Also to lure new, more profitable customers, many of whom are not U.S. residents, by providing the best available customer service". Though this strategy sounds simple and straight forward, this is something which many legacy companies were unable to provide. The usual electronic tickets and online check in is not enough, so they built a robust IT system which helps them create automated tools for improving the efficiency and lead the airlines towards profitability. Let's trace the path of the simple but efficient and sure succeeding.

Eventually except Continental all carriers, had to cut airfares dramatically to maintain the revenue and to overcome the fear of the public. As a matter of fact the average domestic fare was reduced by 16% in 2005 when compared to 2000. This turned out to be a short term solution which backfired. The tickets sales increased, but unexpectedly the oil prices also increased. To reduce the cost nearly all international airlines based in U.S. chose to downsize; reduced the number of flights, abandoned loss giving routes and cancelled orders for new planes. The desperate airline executives even removed the pillows and scraped the paint off the surface of their planes to decrease the weight of the plane and save fuel. (D'Agostino, 2006)

But Continental Airlines chose not to follow this path, they serve meal in their flights even now, and the paint is still on the surface. D'Agostino (2006) cites that "In fact, Continental managed to expand its routes in 2005, by 34 percent, and in 2006 served 288 destinations from its hubs in Newark, N.J., Houston, Cleveland and Guam—more than any other airline in the world. The commitment shown towards customer service has helped earn the airlines numerous awards. For example, Fortune magazine, which for the third consecutive year named

Continental the No. 1 most admired global airline". When almost all of its competitors were complaining, how did Continental airlines was able to retain their dignity and image?

Company executives realized that the mercurial, low fare customers are not their bread and butter, because these consumers have a tendency to switch to whoever offers the cheapest price, and Continental Airlines decided not to follow suit and reduce the fares. Instead, Continental's management decided to focus on attracting loyal customers who are willing to pay more for better quality and sophistication. D'Agostino (2006) cites "Continental slowly changed itself under a strategy voiced by Bethune as 'Worst to First'. Bethune upgraded the company's fleet of aircraft and reorganized its management structure". (Say for example, typically your bosses determine your bonuses, but Continental chose to do the reverse, the subordinates assess the bosses' performance and that determines the bonus for the upper management. This helped them to ease their labour relations.)

Then in 2002, Bethune progressed even further and launched the next mantra "First to Favourite." Also the CRM system which they had was identified to be disparate. D'Agostino (2006) cites that, "They created a new cross-enterprise data warehouse that is fed by more than 25 enterprise systems; it includes schedules, reservations, customer profiles and demographics, airline maintenance, employee and crew payroll, and customer care".

This system helps create a 360 degree view of each customer and provides programs like Continental's OnePass or Elite frequent-flier which includes the member which counts to 31 million customers. This kind of creative database has helped company executives to ascertain and it is called the CVM (customer value metric). This CVM figure assigned for each and every customer helps them to account the price spent by every customer and also the cost for airlines to fly the passenger. This information helps the airline determine the value of each customer to their business. D'Agostino (2006) explains, "The CVM is calculated each month on a scale of 1 to 100, effectively stratifying frequent fliers into tiers of profitability. But the CVM means nothing if it isn't put to good use. When the Continental Airlines feeds the data into its day-to-day systems, it can accommodate high-value customers appropriately.

It's about building relationships with the loyal customers so that they will fly the same Continental Airlines every time."

How does the CVM System work? D'Agostino (2006) explains the methodology in a detailed manner, "One instance is if a flight is more than 1.5 hours late then the system sends an automated e-mail to the top privileged customers on that particular flight apologizing for the delay from the customer relations. Also, the best customers get rewards, like frequent-flier miles, for the inconvenience caused. This single program increased the retaining of customers by 8% which is quite significant. The CVM ratings calculated by the IT system is used to give special privileges to specific customers and to retain them to the brand. This includes access to private lounges, head-of-line boarding, first-off-the-carousel baggage handling, and attempts to honour seat preferences." Obviously the loyal Customers are the main cash producers. With these kind of programs the Continental reduced the defection rate to as low as 2% which is quite low in such a competitive industry.

Progressively, the second agenda they had was to look out and create new business. Continental had another simple plan: Attract and Impress normal travellers into its exclusive frequent-flier programs with numerous tech-based perks generated by their automated system; then convince them to become loyal to their brand. D'Agostino (2006) cites an executive explains, "For example, travellers who enrol in the OnePass program can take advantage of a new service called Trip Alert, which sends SMS notifications about upcoming flights. In the near future, the system will also assist passengers who have missed a connection. So as soon as the passenger lands and turns on their phone, they'll get a message from Trip Alert with their new flight information. Then they can print out their new boarding pass in a nearby kiosk". Such a wonderful innovation it would be.

But just as important is in gathering information about the routes which produce the most loyal and profitable customers. The investment in the business intelligence tools and call-centre monitoring software has resulted in Continental's growing destination list. The main reason for Continental's technology success can be attributed to the carrier's stand against outsourcing. The company's IT tech staffs handle just about everything without any outsourcing.

In spite of pits and falls, Continental Airlines executives say "We are confident that is on the right course. In the first quarter of 2006, the company reduced its losses to $66 million when compared with $186 million a year back. And they are certain that profitability is not far". At the moment Continental is in the best position than any other lines and will lead the path for recovery.

What we can learn from this case study is that they did not follow the herd totally in more than one ways. When other airlines were beating around the bush by cutting the fares, Continental Airlines did not lose focus and indulge in steps for quick recovery. Instead they supplemented the competitors' market. When the competitors cut quality and fares, Continental airlines supplemented them by high quality and high fares. Introducing loyalty benefits for their customers helped them to retain a large chunk of customer base by improving quality for their best deserved customers. Innovation went hand in hand with technology which paid off very well as expected. But, other airlines may follow suite of this innovation, so Continental Airlines should be dynamic and flexible to change its strategies accordingly.

The next innovative step they took was not to outsource the IT department fully. Since the company's stakes and problems are more relevant to their own employees than contract employees, this was a wise decision and paid off well. Also, this helped them create proprietary software which is unique and genuine to their brand. This can become an important insight for many companies that are outsourcing to Asian countries to take the benefit of exchange rate, where the failure rate can be as significant as 30%.

It is always interesting to investigate the successful changes that have happened in an organization and link it to theories put forth by experts. Experts believe that the "Broadest most abstract things to change are vision and culture". Regarding the change in Continental Airlines, Vision which is the most conceptual and is created by re-thinking and re-conceiving usually by the leader geared the change. Also specific changes in the products and people were also mobilized. If we try to figure out the kind of change, we can find that it is a combination of Planned Change, Driven Change and Evolved Change. The management realized that there is a crisis and the issues faced are fundamental and they pioneered the innovation defined by ChanKim and Mauborgne (Value Innovation). Their focus of change was not just the competitor but it was the customer. So, they managed change successfully by innovation and not imitation.

The Corporate Recovery strategies are not just for companies which are under crisis, Even a seemingly healthy company can become insolvent in a matter of weeks. Since prevention is better than cure, foresight in management is really important in the day to day business to avoid future crisis situation. Each and every employee of the company should realize that Efforts will never fail and we are in this world to put effective quality efforts in right place.

This case study has provided a foundation for future work. Although many valuable insights were revealed through this study, there is an ongoing opportunity for future research in the area of service quality, failure and recovery, as well as the service quality gaps within the airline industry.

References

Author not mentioned (2004), *"Dark skies: Can the airlines bounce back from the brink"*
Strategic Direction [0258-0543] vol:20 iss:1 pg:10 -12 Retrieved 27th Jan 2008, from World Wide Web (Available for Athens users at) http://www.emeraldinsight.com/Insight/viewPDF.jsp?Filename=html/Output/Published/EmeraldFullTextArticle/Pdf/0560200103.pdf

David Bamford, Tatiana Xystouri (2005), *"A case study of service failure and recovery within an international airline"*, Managing Service Quality, Vol. 15 No. 3, pp. 306-322

Retrieved 27th Jan 2008, from World Wide Web (Available for Athens users at)
http://www.emeraldinsight.com/Insight/viewContentItem.do;jsessionid=EA06CE63A9D16E9E9110ACE7F6036ADE?contentType=Article&contentId=1503755

David Elliott (2007), *"Corporate Recovery"*, Retrieved 27th Jan 2008, from World Wide Web at http://www.accaglobal.com/students/study_exams/qualifications/acca_choose/acca/professional/ba/technical_articles/2951310

Don Amerman (2008), "Gordon M. Bethune – Chairman and Chief Executive Officer Continental Airlines", Retrieved 27th Jan 2008, from World Wide Web at http://www.answers.com/topic/gordon-bethune?cat=biz-fin

Debra D'Agostino (2006), "Case Study: Continental Airline's Tech Strategy Takes Off", Retrieved 27th Jan 2008, from World Wide Web at http://www.cioinsight.com/article2/0,1397,1989438,00.asp

Slatter, Stuart St. P. (1984) "Corporate recovery: a guide to turnaround management", Harmondsworth: Penguin

Susan Combs (2002) "Keep 'em Flying", Retrieved 27th Jan 2008, from World Wide Web at http://www.window.state.tx.us/comptrol/fnotes/fn0205/keeping.html

Susan E. Jackson, Randall S. Schuler, (2004), "Managing Human Resources Through Strategic Partnerships" Retrieved 27th Jan 2008, from World Wide Web at
http://books.google.com/books?id=wdgzWha5angC&printsec=frontcover&dq=continental+airlines+cinderella%27s+midnight#PPA33,M1

CROSS CULTURAL MANAGEMENT

CHAPTER – VIII

CROSS CULTURAL MANAGEMENT

1.0) Introduction:

The world has become a global village because of the advancements in transportation and communication. Information Technology has shrunk the world like never seen before with email, internet and, increasingly, teleconferencing providing swift links between people in organizations in different countries. At the same time more and more companies are seeking an international presence as a means of diversifying their markets. For example, the economies of South-East Asia have attracted massive investment from other countries and have also, in turn, invested heavily in Europe and Americas. In such a situation we need to emphasize the behavioural aspects of management.

In order to work in a multicultural environment, we need to have increased awareness of cross-cultural issues, and to learn constructive approach to international co-operation. For this study, we have chosen the countries India, United Kingdom and France. The proposed situation is to find the cultural profiling needed for an Indian company to participate in an International Project with United Kingdom and France. The reason for choosing these three countries mainly because India has recently become an important site for investments and, many foreign countries started viewing India as a potential global player. Also, India has been a colony of both UK and France and hence the commonalities and differences are prone to be there. Diversity is the one true thing we all have in common. Let's explore it academically.

2.0) Cultural Profiling:

Culture has been defined as "shared patterns of behaviour" as proposed by anthropologist Margaret Mead. However there are over 164 different definitions. Let's see some of the aspects of culture.

2.1) Language:

More than 300 million people in the world speak English and the rest, it sometimes seems, try to. For non-English speakers everywhere, English has become the common tongue. Even in France, the most determinedly non-English speaking nation in the world, the war against English encroachment has largely been lost (Bryson, 1996). The statistics of English as a language in the World Today (Guy and Mattock, 1993, Pg 131) is given below:

- 300 million speak English as their mother tongue
- 800 million more put it to use daily
- 75% of the world's mail is in English
- 80% of the data stored on the world's computers
- 45% of the world's scientific publications

There are now more non-native speakers of English than there are native speakers. In India in terms of numbers of English speakers, the Indian subcontinent ranks third in the world, after the USA and UK. An estimated 4% of the Indian population uses English; although the number might seem small, out of the total population that is about 35 million people (Crystal, 1995:101). But only a minimal fraction of the English-using Indian population has any interaction with native speakers of English (Hohenthal, 1998).

Even types of English dialect or accent can be perceived quite negatively such that business success is jeopardized. The bland assumption that if people can speak English and make themselves understood, business can then proceed effectively is a long way from the reality where a multitude of distortions, misconceptions and misunderstandings can very easily ruin what otherwise could be a smooth and effective translation or business relationship (Bloch and Starks, 1999).

2.2)   Religion:

In UK, Campbell (2007) says that the Christian aid charity that commissioned the survey report of religion in UK demonstrates the prevalence and potential of prayer and that more people would pray about issues such as world poverty and climate change.

The main religions of the French are Catholicism (62%), Islam (6%), Protestantism (2%) and Judaism (1%), while 26% of the French report that they have no religious affiliation. The same survey showed that 41% of the French think that the existence of God is unlikely or impossible and 58% think that it is certain or probable.

According to Saheli (2001) Hinduism is the largest major religion in India. Approximately 80% of the population practices various forms of Hinduism. The Mughals brought Islam with them when they invaded India in the 12th century. Today, Islam is practiced by about 14% of the population. 2.4% of the population are Christians (mostly found on the southwest coastal areas and in the northeast). 2% are Sikhs (found principally in the Punjab, although many migrated to Delhi after partition)

2.3)   High Context and Low Context Communication:

The general terms "high context" and "low context" (popularized by Edward Hall) are used to describe broad-brush cultural differences between societies (Beer, 2003)

a) High Context (Beer, 2003):

- Less verbally explicit communication, less written/formal information

- More internalized understandings of what is communicated

- Multiple cross-cutting ties and intersections with others

- Long term relationships

- Strong boundaries- who is accepted as belonging vs. who is considered an "outsider"

- Knowledge is situational, relational.

- Decisions and activities focus around personal face-to-face relationships, often around a central person who has authority.

b) Low Context (Beer, 2003):

- Rule oriented, people play by external rules

- More knowledge is codified, public, external, and accessible.

- Sequencing, separation--of time, of space, of activities, of relationships

- More interpersonal connections of shorter duration

- Knowledge is more often transferable

- Task-centred. Decisions and activities focus around what needs to be done, division of responsibilities.

Hall, E. and M. Hall (1990), as cited by Wortz (2005) affirm that, Indians communicate in a high context way and France and United Kingdom communicate in low context way.

2.4) Hofstede's Model(Hofstede, 2001):

In his survey of IBM employees, Hofstede used a questionnaire containing about 150 questions of which 20 were used to create four value dimensions along which he compared the national cultures in his sample. The four dimensions are Power Distance, Uncertainty Avoidance, Individualism-Collectivism, Masculinity-Femininity. These four dimensions are defined as below:

a) Power Distance: It is the vertical Dependency Relationship which reflects sub-ordinates fear of expressing disagreement with managers. Lower Power Distance denotes decentralization, lower concentration of authority and flatter organizations. Higher Power Distance means Centralization, Higher Concentration of Authority and Taller organization.

b) Uncertainty Avoidance: The need for predictability and written rules. Lower Uncertainty Avoidance indicates less structuring of activities, Emotional need for fewer written rules and more generalists. Higher Uncertainty Avoidance signify more structuring of activities, emotional need for more rules and more specialists

c) Individualism and Collectivism: Horizontal Dependency of individuals on the group. Collectivism represents relationship based on Personal

Trust, promotion by Ascription and work/home diffusely related. Individualism corresponds to relations based around contracts and transactions, promotion by merit and work/home specific and separate.

d) Masculine and feminine Culture: The extent to which values are more Masculine (assertive, competitive, tough, results-oriented) or Feminine (modest, co-operative, nurturing, tender, equity-oriented). This may affect how conflict is resolved and also might influence motivational approaches.

Geert Hofstede later added a fifth Dimension after conducting an additional international study with a survey instrument developed with Chinese employees and managers which is the Short Term and Long Term Orientation.

The comparative scores for India, United Kingdom and France are given below

	Dimensions	Power Distance		Individualism		Uncertainty Avoidance		Masculinity		Long Term Orientation	
Countries	India	77		48		40		56		61	
	United Kingdom	35		89		35		66		25	
	France	68		71		86		43			
Differences in Dimensions	**India and UK**	42	Red	41	Red	5	Green	20	Amber	36	Red
	UK and France	33	Red	18	Amber	53	Red	23	Red	N/A	
	France and India	9	Green	23	Red	46	Red	13	Amber	N/A	

Differences < 10 = **Green** = Similar, hence can be ignored

Differences > 10 & < 20 = **Amber** = Needs a little bit of extra management

Differences > 20 = **Red** = Needs a lot of training and caution before business starts

2.5)   Trompenaars' Model:

Trompenaars (1994) identified seven important dimensions on which cultures disagree. Faced with an existential question or basic dilemma of being, they go opposite ways. The seven dilemmas are as follows:

a) Universalism vs. Particularism: The relative salience of rules (universal) or exceptions (particulars).

b) Analyzed Specifics vs. Integrated wholes: Are we more effective as managers when we analyze phenomena into specifics i.e. parts, facts, targets or when we integrate and configure such details into diffused patterns, relationships and wider context.

c) Individualism vs. Communitarianism: Is it more important to focus upon the enhancement of each individual, his or her rights, motivations, rewards, capacities etc. or should more attention be paid to advancement of a corporation as a community.

d) Inner-directed vs. outer-directed orientation: Which are the more important guides to action, or inner-directed judgments, decisions and commitments, or signals, demands and trends in the outside world to which we may adjust?

e) Time as sequence vs. time as synchronization: Is it more important to do things fast, in the shortest possible sequence of passing time, or to synchronize all efforts, just-in-time, so that completion is coordinated?

f) Achieved status vs. Ascribed: Should the status of employees depend on what they achieved and how they have achieved and how they have performed, or on some other characteristic important to the corporation, i.e. age, seniority, gender, education, potential, strategic role?

g) Equality vs. Hierarchy: Is it more important that we treat employees as equals so as to elicit from them the best they have to give, or to emphasize the judgment and the authority of the hierarchy that is coaching and evaluating them?

Based on surveys with dilemmatic situations questionnaire done by Trompenaars (1993) the following are the results:

	United Kingdom	France	India
Universalism vs. Particularism	90 (more universal)	68 (more universal)	59 (more universal)
Specifics vs. whole or diffuse	82 (more specific)	81 (more specific)	46 (more diffuse)
Individuality vs. Community	66 (more independent)	48 (more communal)	61 (more independent)
Inner vs. Outer-Directed	66 (more inner)	50 (in the middle)	36 (more outer)
Time as sequential vs. Synch.	Past and Present overlap well, but present and future overlap slightly	Slightly overlapping past with present and present future	Not available
Achievement vs. Ascription of status	47 (more ascription)	27 (more ascription)	26 (more ascription)
Equality vs. Hierarchy	Flatter	Mid sized	Taller

2.5)   CPAS model:

The CPAS model has been used in management workshops, both to assess the cultural profiles of participants and to provide a means for evaluation of likely cultural conflicts and synergies between workshop groups and the commercial geography in which they operate. This model takes into account both the Hofstede's dimensions and the Trompenaar's dimensions and it is indicated in the table below.

The data in this model for India is not yet available. However the figures for United Kingdom and France will give the Indian managers an idea of the cultural inclination of these 2 countries. Also, the Ambiguity orientation figures are yet to come, the study is in progress.

Model	Orientation	Bias Cultural variant	Group Cultural Bias From 0 to 100	UK	France
H	Time	Strategic Horizon	Short to Long Term	18	49
T	Emotion	Expression of emotion	Expressive to Controlled	78	9
H	Hierarchies	Hierarchical orientation	Democratic to Bureaucratic	46	85
T	Work Relationship	Relationship orientation	Context specific to Broad	9	18
T	Status	Status orientation	Achievement to Ascription	27	49
T	Profit and Social	Profit orientation	Profit to Social	31	88
T	Systems	Systems orientation	Rational to Humanist	32	93
H	Ambiguity	Study in Progress			
T	Rules	Rule Orientation	Adherence to Interpreting	40	93
T	Control	Control orientation	Assertive to Reactive	32	27
H	Gender	Gender Orientation	Masculine to Feminine	32	58
H	Group	Group Orientation	Individualist to Collectivist	29	58

H – Hofstede's dimension

T – Trompenaars' dimension

3.0) Management Styles:

Management Style is the way in which a manager work, motivate, show themselves, perceive counterparts, meeting etiquettes, oblige hierarchy, their priorities and strategy making capacity. The management style is also linked directly to the local culture. So, it is obvious that geographically apart nations exhibit different management styles.

3.1)　United Kingdom:

The British management style can be described as given below (Barsoux and Lawrence, 1990)

1. The British managers are considered to be "Jack of all trades". The idea is that with a little common sense the Britons can manage anything. British managers are managerially conscious.
2. In terms of personal exchanges, British managers are informal, they don't keep their jackets, or tie their tie tight or their sleeves unrolled.
3. British managers are consciously political in their actions. They take pride in showing off their ability to shape, influence and decide in informal ways.
4. They are in a way humanitarian – they take people as the point of reference, rather than system objectives.
5. The readiness to joke even about business matters is distinctively British.
6. Britain is persuasion oriented. British managers want to get their own way, but they want to persuade people into it with their manipulative skills mentioned above.
7. When it comes to strategy orientation, the British brand of strategy is intuitive.

3.2)　France:

The following are based on the work of Michael Crozier on work relations in a bureaucratic context in France (Barsoux and Lawrence, 1998)

1. More formal working atmosphere, with relative absence of joking around.
2. The Executive behaviour is restrained even when they climb up the career ladder.
3. They do not tend to appreciate inquiries into their personal

lives, their family circumstances or how they spend their weekend.

4. The French are very sensitive to actions which risk encroaching on their freedom – even if the initiative is claimed to be for the 'greater good'

5. The French cadres like to have a territory to call their own in their office. They prefer working in isolation and social openness is at a very low level.

6. French managers like to talk. In meetings, they have no qualms about advancing the discussion on several fronts at once.

7. They see time as expandable. They do not expect the clock to control events.

8. Hierarchy is distinctive and segregation could also be seen in existence at most companies of separate canteens for workers and management.

3.3)   India:

It's an unpleasant truth that with the rich cultural heritage of India, the quest for an Indian paradigm of management is still on (Pradip Bhattacharya, 2005). The Indian managers try to ape the western management style working right at random. They struggle between their value-driven lives and to meet the business objectives. The values rooted in the deep-structure of Indian culture and society which influence the management styles of managers (Chakraborty, 1991) are:

1. The Individual Must be respected
2. Co-operation and trust
3. Jealousy is harmful for mental health
4. Purification of the Mind
5. Top-quality Product/Service in some areas where the revenue is more
6. Work-is-Worship
7. Containment of greed
8. Ethico-moral soundness
9. Self discipline and Self restraint
10. Customer satisfaction to some extent
11. Creativity

12. Inspiration to give
13. Renunciation and Detachment

4.0) Recommendations:

The following are the recommendations arrived from study that has been done here.

a. Learning the nuances of French language which is to differentiate "Tu" (familiar) and "Vous" (Formal), also knowing the local language will break the initial ice before any negotiations.

b. All the three countries chosen have a secular government and outlook. Still meetings on Sundays must be avoided. And for Indians, they should restraint from their religious marks on the forehead and appear neutral and formal during meetings and in office.

c. More than understanding whether the communication is low context or high context, the managers should confirm their understandings of communication through detailed, clear-cut, well written e-mails to their foreign counterparts periodically to avoid mishaps.

d. Also, in communication, half information is very dangerous; there should not be any lag between what one believes and the actual truth.

e. The difference in Uncertainty Avoidance between India and France is very high according to the Hofstede's model. So, any interaction should be without any ambiguity.

f. The difference of Power Distance figures for UK and India is very high, so the Indian high level managers can expect some uncomfortable feedbacks right on the face. They should equip themselves to face such a situation.

g. The Individualism figures for both France and UK are very high, so they are not going to like any agenda which proposes group work.

5.0)   Conclusion:

"The end of all exploring will be to arrive where we started and know the place for the first time" – T.S. Eliot

The conclusion is that "Diversity is the one true thing we all have in common", which was mentioned in the Introduction. But now we can see that in a different light. To develop tolerance for differences, learning tendency, humanity in perception and ethical behaviour will definitely take us to an elite status. So, let's be part of a global civilization.

References:

Barsoux, Jean-Louis and Lawrence, Peter (1997), *French Management Elitism in Action* .Wiltshire: Casell Publishing (Pg 84 – 102)

Barsoux, Jean-Louis and Lawrence, Peter (1990), *The Challenge of British Management.* Singapore: Macmillan Press (Pg 106 - 121)

Beer, Jennifer E., (1997-2003), *High and Low Context*, Retrieved 13th Nov 2007, from World Wide Web http://www.culture-at-work.com/highlow.html

Bhattacharya, Pradip 2005, Book Reviews, *The Quest for an Indian Paradigm of Management*, Retrieved 13th Nov 2007, from the World Wide Web http://www.boloji.com/bookreviews/061.htm

Bill, Bryson (1996), *Mother Tongue : English & How It Got That Way*, Retrieved 14th Nov 2007, from World Wide Web http://www.northshire.com/siteinfo/bookinfo.php?isbn=0-380-71543-0&item=0

Bloch, Brian and Starks, Donna 1999. *The many faces of English: intra-language variation and its implications for international business. Corporate communications, [Online].* Vol. 4 (Iss. 2), Retrieved 13th Nov 2007, from World Wide Web (Available for Athens users at) http://www.emeraldinsight.com/Insight/viewContentItem.do?contentType=Article&contentId=857962

Campbell, Denis 2007. *A third of adults believe God watches over them.* The Observer 11 Nov., Retrieved 13th Nov 2007, from World Wide Web http://www.guardian.co.uk/religion/Story/0,,2209245,00.html

Guy, Vincent & Mattock, John (1993) *THE New INTERNATIONAL MANAGER – An Action Guide for Cross-Cultural Business,* 2nd Ed. Bucks: Kogan Page

Hofstede, Geert (2001), Geert Hofstede™ *Cultural Dimensions,*

Retrieved 14th Nov 2007, from World Wide Web http://www.geert-hofstede.com/

Hohenthal, Annika (1998) *English in India -- and Who Speaks English to Whom and When?*, [Online] Retrieved 14th Nov 2007, from the World Wide Web http://www.languageinindia.com/may2003/annika.html

S.K.Chakraborty 1991, *Management by Values- Towards Cultural Congruence* Delhi: Oxford University Press (Pg 19,20)

Saheli, 2001, *Religion in India*, Retrieved 13th Nov 2007, http://www.judypat.com/india/temple.htm

Würtz, E. (2005). *A cross-cultural analysis of websites from high-context cultures and low-context cultures.* Journal of Computer-Mediated Communication, 11(1), article 13. Retrieved 13th Nov 2007, from World Wide Web http://jcmc.indiana.edu/vol11/issue1/wuertz.html

PEOPLE MANAGEMENT

CHAPTER – IX

DOWNSIZING AND ORGANIZATIONAL CULTURE

It is always painful for both employee and employer to make someone redundant in order to downsize. Though it is obvious that the employee feels bad but in many cases the employer also feels bad because of the emotional bond that has been built by the employee, working *with* the company and not *for* the company (Tiorio). We intend to conduct a study about the change in organizational culture because of downsizing.

Organizational culture pervades everywhere in the organization and hence difficult to be defined exactly and put into analysis. However it is possible to study some of the elements of culture. Here we are going to see the possible effects on the culture of the organization because of downsizing. Downsizing is defined as "falls into the category of management tools for achieving desired change, much like "rightsizing" and "reengineering"" (Hickok, 1998).

Many scholars have defined organizational culture as the shared beliefs and values guiding the thinking and behavioural styles of employees. This includes the important issues and goals that are shared by most members of the organization as well as pervasive group behaviour norms. The shared values of the whole organization is considered to be less visible and not so easy to change but the group behaviour norms form the sub-culture of the organization and is considered to be more visible and easier to change (Lankford, Mintu-Wimsatt, 1999).

The chosen organization is DTU which is Dominion Travelogics Unlimited, a company that survived a major corporate reorganization (Applebaum *et al*, 1998).

The employees of DTU were part of the culture they helped to create for as long as they had been working there. But when the management decided to reorganize, the employees felt that their freedom was lost. Also, policies, rules and regulations were changed which threatened their association to the company rather than help them cope up with the loss. The social events and value recognition programs for employees were cancelled because of major cuts in the budget. This resulted in significant drop in the motivation of employees. Salaries were frozen for the past 3 years which also stopped them from hiring new employees to replace the laid off employees. As a result, in many sections, the job load increased manifold and no appropriate monetary compensation was offered (Applebaum *et al*, 1998).

The main problem for DTU was to transform into a more performing company culturally than what it was, so as to meet the goals of both the company and the employees. The relevant issues were (Applebaum *et al*, 1998):

- Examine the specific problem areas in the current culture;

- Identify the techniques needed to address the current problems in the culture;

- Recommend the techniques to be used and also suggest a feasible time frame to implement the changes and also insist the need for feedback measures;

- The management was ready to accept the feedback measures which are obtained by research about the downsized companies;

- The employer and the employees mutually understand the significance of human assets.

In this context the sub-culture is that of the survivors who are caught in fear, low in morale and low in cohesions. There was a belief that re-engineering, restructuring, delayering and downsizing are influential management paradigms. But Morden (1997) contends that this contemporary paradigm is flawed, and in need of extensive qualification.

Morden (1997) also cites Kanter's justification for downsizing has the following benefits:

- restructuring to achieve smaller and more flexible structures of organization and management, which should be capable of doing more with less;

- making increasing use of co-operation and partnership within the value chain;

- the encouragement of innovation and entrepreneurship.

These are counteracted by Morden (1997) that the style of management after downsizing is perceived by the employees to be authoritative and exploitative and there is an increase in the responsibilities and personal work load taken by the employees and the higher officers are considered to be less and less trust worthy. Due to lack of trust, the leadership is badly eroded and seen as short termist, negative role model, lack credibility and failure to protect the sub-ordinates. The middle managers ultimately may become the scapegoat, acting as a target for negative or aggressive sentiments, blame, and frustration on the part of both redundant employees and the survivor employees. The concept of motivation also changes direction, it becomes an issue of fear and survival.

After downsizing a survey was conducted (Appelbaum *et al*, 1998) to measure the organizational climate in the aftermath of the downsizing. Though it was assured that the content will remain confidential, employees should have feared about being really confidential. Anyway, the survey results showed that the morale of the employees ended up in dissatisfaction. When they had to downsize, the DTU management never communicated the exact reasons, methods and, this left an impression that they themselves were not sure where they are heading in the future. But it is also true that many employees agreed that downsizing is essential but also felt it was not handled the way it should have. They did not announce the guidelines they are looking for in the profiles of employees who are to be labelled as redundant. Also, those employees were not informed prior to their firing. The dissatisfaction was mainly based on the irony that some of the employees who were laid off should have stayed and some of those who stayed should have laid off. If they had released the guidelines for the downsizing this could have been easily avoided. The communication was the main problem, because the employees were kept in dark until the last hour, which caused a lot of stress on the employees. This gave way for the rumours to go around and spoiled the working environment and eventually the morale of all the employees.

The employees believed that the relationship with the employer was long-term and stable, but after the downsizing, it changed to more short-term and contingent in order to accommodate layoffs (Hickok, 1998).

The cultural mind set of the leader when it comes to downsizing is an important part to be studied and analyzed. In all cases the downsizing results in a negative cultural change which might act as an organizational destabilizer. Whether this cultural change causes benefits to the company or not is left to individual's speculation. The resultant short term effects and long term consequences have to be answered by course of time. The companies with lesser bureaucracies give freedom for employees to make them work and interact more positively. The impact of the loyalty of employees and the emotional bond between the employee and employer which is accrued over time in the tenure of the employment is left to the judgment of time (Hickok, 1998).

Any organization will have a flexibility plan about how to reduce the personnel expenses when the need arises. Important decisions about downsizing employees inflict pain on the employees and destroy the congruent environmental culture built by the employees. But there are certain methods that can be adopted for downsizing which reinforces or leave alone the current culture. This is distinguished from the methods which cause negative culture in the Table 1. The chosen methods which are less disruptive and in fact reinforces a positive culture where employees feel a sense of control are labelled as reinforcing practices and those methods which are not handled properly and induces pain among the work force particularly to those who are asked to leave are considered to be destabilizing (Hickok, 1998).

So, it is in the hands of the top management how to identify, communicate and compensate the employees who are chosen to leave and those chosen not to leave. Job is in most cases pays the livelihood for the whole family, so it has to be dealt with a moral approach. So, it is not just going to affect the individual but also all those people who are dependent on them. So, the transition should be handled with utmost humanity to avoid the disenfranchisement felt by the survivors. The exact individuals to be fired have to be kept confidential to give a chance to make it seem that they leave gracefully among their colleagues. Also, immediately after a lay off, the work load of individuals will increase, so that should be compensated by social events which will energize employees to do work more effectively. A positive culture cannot happen overnight, it takes quite a long time to happen and longer time to identify that change in culture.

Table 1

Culture Reinforcing and Culture Destabilizing Practices
Distinguished (Hickok, 1998)

CULTURE REINFORCING	CULTURE DESTABILIZING
Voluntary reductions (e.g., attrition, buyouts, job sharing)	Involuntary reductions (layoffs)
Advance notice about termination.	Sudden termination
Shared pain (e.g., cuts across all levels) avoiding scapegoats.	Winners/losers (e.g., executives get big bonuses while cutting others' positions)
Explicit criteria for "who stays, who goes" and communicated well in advance	Criteria are secret
Transition assistance for those who have to depart involuntarily	Little or no assistance
Transition assistance for survivors	Little or no assistance
New "rules of engagement" between organizations are made clear, the goals are set and more communication channels are created.	Reductions treated as exception or something which does not require explanation
Participation in direction-setting from various levels in organization	Goal setting done at top without input

In the process of downsizing, the following should be included (Hickok, 1998): ensuring the fundamental decency of the approach being considered, engaging in appropriate dialogue, thinking through the consequences for those who may be adversely affected, having ready explanations for multiple constituencies, and offering a realistic opportunity for a better future for the organization and the organization's stakeholders.

As markets get saturated in the developed nations, and the advantages of outsourcing, the job cutting has been going rounds for a while. The author suspects if there is at least one instance where layoff was well received by the employees. But definitely shrewd foresight on the part of the top management can avoid a lot of mishaps in downsizing. The author is sure that in the long run in some companies there would have been positive impact on the financial figures of the company. What about the employees who have put their hard work for the company? It poses more questions than answers, like what is the bond between the employer and employee? Is it just monetary, or is there something in there when you wish "Good Morning" to your boss when you meet him in the morning. Let's think a little deep on it when we wish them the next time.

REFERENCES

Appelbaum, S. H., Leblanc, M., Shapiro, B. T. (1998). The aftermath of downsizing – A case study of disengagement, disidentification, disenfranchisement and disenchantment. Journal of Management Development. *17(6), 402-431. [Available for Athens users at]* http://www.emeraldinsight.com/Insight/ViewContentServlet?Filename=Published/EmeraldFullTextArticle/Articles/0260170602.html *[Accessed on 23-03-08]*

Goodman E. C. (Editor) (1997). The Forbes Book of Business Quotations. New York: Tess Press. Pg. 242.

Lankford W., Mintu-Wimsatt A. (1999) Another look at corporate America's culture. *Career Development International.* 4(2), 88-93. [Available for Athens Users at] http://www.emeraldinsight.com/Insight/ViewContentServlet?Filename=Published/EmeraldFullTextArticle/Articles/1370040203.html [Accessed on 23-03-08]

Hickok T. A. (1998). Downsizing and Organizational Culture. Public Administration and Management – An Interactive Journal. *Volume 3 Number 3* [online journal] http://www.pamij.com:80/hickok.html *[Accessed on 23-03-08]*

Morden T. (1997). A strategic evaluation of re-engineering, restructuring, delayering and downsizing policies as flawed paradigm. *Management Decision.* 35(3), 240-249. [Available for Athens users at] http://www.emeraldinsight.com/Insight/ViewContentServlet?Filename=Published/EmeraldFullTextArticle/Articles/0010350307.html [Accessed on 23-03-08]

CHAPTER – X

BUILDING THE NEW NIC

1. INTRODUCTION:

The problem at hand in the fictitious 'Northampton Insurance Company (NIC)' is that they need a cultural make over in order to modernise, reduce friction and stay ahead which is something very common in any kind of business. It is the necessity of time where the successful realise that change is one thing that never changes. One of the main advantages that NIC has is that the management have realised that change needs to be done in order to sustain their position which is the first step of success. The intention of this report is to provide NIC with a wholesome HR strategy in order to help them implement the change they want.

2. SWOT ANALYSIS:

The Strengths, Weaknesses, Opportunities and Threats of NIC are listed with whatever information is available and analysed so as to help them and come up with appropriate strategies.

2.1. Strengths (Internal):

a. The management have understood that the culture of the organization needs to be changed in order to keep itself up to date and show to its customers a modern and positive attitude.

b. The NIC is still one of the largest financial services organizations in UK.

c. It has got seven million customers.

d. The income in 2006 was £3.73 billion with assets under management of £32 billion.

2.2. Weaknesses (Internal):

a. The old ways of management which is male dominated, hierarchical and status orientated.

b. The management style has been described as bullying (especially about women), coercive and dominated by a cult of personality.

c. Petty things like, should not wear high heels, because carpet will get spoiled and men have to wear jackets when they move between floors are restricted.

d. The higher official (executives) have their own suite and separate dining facilities.

2.3. Opportunities (External):

a. They can modernize and inject new culture by following other companies who have done that in the past.

b. Proper training activities are available to empower employees.

c. Find out ways in which the customer base can be expanded.

d. Modernise and reduce differences with the parent company so that communication and coordination flourishes.

2.4.   **Threats (External):**

a.   The NIC might lose its virtue, position and customer base if it starts being reactive rather than pro active.

b.   The differences between NIC and its parent retail bank seem to have increased and it is right now an insular approach which might cause a lot of unnecessary problems.

c.   The NIC is right now facing problems in attracting and retaining staff which might end up in losing potential employees to competitors.

d.   The customer base is almost exclusively concentrated among low-income households who may switch to competitors if they are offered cheaper options.

2.5.   **Strategies from SWOT Analysis:**

a.   Hire an external consultant to analyze the situation and come up with strategies in order to transform NIC, which they have done.

b.   The NIC is a financially rich company so that, they can schedule training programs for the staffs in order to empower them to cope up with the changing needs and for better customer service approaches.

c.   Since, the NIC has a strong customer base it can be used to build CRM software to serve the customer better.

d.   Customer loyalty schemes can be introduced to retain the customers.

e.   Social Activities can be arranged between the employees of NIC and the parent retail bank so that differences are identified and resolved.

f.   The NIC is in fact pro active than reactive and it has to develop HR skills in forecasting the possible problems.

g.   NIC is still one of the largest financial services, so it can use that position to experiment a little, by introducing a very attractive package for new skilled employees and retain the existing potential employees and use them effectively.

h.   To capture high income customers, a celebrity brand ambassador can be contracted and marketing strategies can be inclined towards high income customers.

i.   To get rid of the dress and shoes issues, NIC can introduce dress-down scheme where people can wear anything they like on one of the days of the week.

j.   The traditional masculine culture can be reduced to by introducing voting system by women as to find out who the best mannered man in the organization is.

k.   One dining hall for the whole organization can avoid hierarchical issues and also have a way when everyone can talk to each other.

l.   In addition to social activities between the NIC and its parent company, common HR policies have to be introduced to the whole company.

m.   Rewarding schemes should be more effective and more frequent to retain staff and to attract new staff.

n.   The shedding of 2500 employees and the closure of 100 district sales and claims offices has to be done smoothly in accordance with the UK legislation.

o.   Introducing some learning programs for employees to develop new skills to give better customer services.

3.　　MANAGING CHANGE:

Self (2007) points out that change in organization has become a cliché and is as much a cliché that there will be resistance to that change. He also cites Armenakis *et al.* (1999) who offers five different elements necessary to create readiness: The need for change, demonstrating that it is the right change, that key people support the change, that members have the confidence they can succeed, and an answer to the question, "What is in it for me/us?"

Self (2007) also says that people perceive change in different ways some with anticipation, some fearful and some ambivalent. They all wait for the cues from the action leader as to what the outcome of the change truly mean. So, the impacts of the change on individuals have to be communicated in a proper manner so that the anomalies in the minds of the individuals are removed. For example in the case of NIC, the shedding of the 2500 jobs has to be handled with utmost care which is dealt separately.

4.　　MODERNISATION PROGRAM:

The modernisation scheme can be called **"Monalisa wears Prada"** which indicates that the goodness of the tradition is maintained with a modern outlook. The major problems of broadening customer base and reduce differences between NIC and the retail bank is dealt separately below.

4.1.　**Learning Culture:**

To develop a positive culture in an organization the employees should realise that learning should never stop and is in fact fun. Barnett (1999) argues that under the super complex conditions of the 'global age' work has to become learning and learning has to become work. He also says that in such conditions, conditions of uncertainty a work has to be presented with infinite learning opportunities. If NIC have to catch up with the changing world, learning should be part of everyday life. Without mentioning Kolb's Learning Cycle we cannot complete Learning Methods. But the knack lies in how to make learning a fun and enjoyable experience in order to attract and retain potential employees.

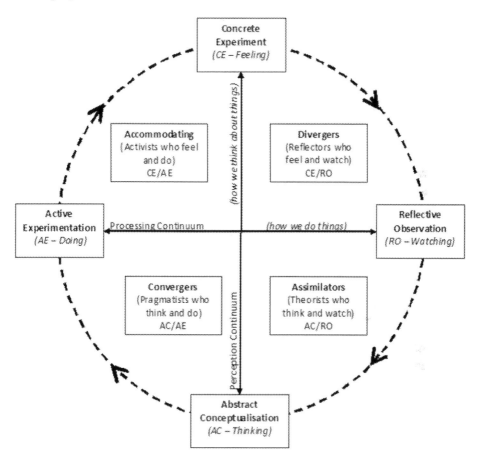

Figure 10.1: Kolb's Learning Cycle

Among the different generations of people, the 'Generation X' people are the most sought after because of the following attributes they possess (Bova and Kroth, 2001):

- They could think parallel

- Act independently and resourceful

- Ready to accept change

- Believe in quick and positive results

- Accept diverse work culture

- Expect to strike a balance between work and life

- Technical literacy is high

- Can be dealt directly by recruiters

- Willing to learn all their life

The study of Generation X employees indicated that three approaches to learning appear to have relevance and application to them (Bova and Kroth, 2001):

1. *Action learning:* This is simply learning by doing and this is not about problem solving this is in fact the learning that happens in the process of finding solutions.

2. *Incidental learning:* This kind of learning is the learning which happens as a by product of doing something. In 1942, McGeough (Bova and Kroth, 2001) defined incidental learning as "learning which apparently takes place without a specific motive or a specified formal instruction and set to learn the specific material in question."

3. *Formal or traditional learning:* This is the least attractive way of learning for the Generation X employees. But they are motivated to training if fun is included in fact fun is in the top of their priorities.

This is basically to retain and attract the cream of the employees, but it is not supposed to deny the contribution made by the older or younger generation of employees. This is just a suggestion for the changes to be implemented in the near future in the organizations. On course of time, the generations will change and obviously the learning practices will also change. People who belong to other generations can also fit in this generation, if they have the relevant learning practices. This is not age discrimination but just following the trend.

4.2. **Empowerment Programs:**

The idea of empowerment is not new it has been in practice from 6th century in China. But the definitions for empowerment have evolved over time due to changes in the environment. Right now, the definitions not just have power but it also includes increase in responsibility in the use of that power. In fact choosing where to focus ones energies can be said to be empowered thinking and the choices are influenced by contextual factors. Also empowerment is an ongoing process and levels of empowerment can be monitored. At times, the decision not to act may be the most empowering choice at that time (Hogan, 2000).

Møller (1994) talks about employeeship, being a good employee to have the following aspects Responsibility, Loyalty and Initiative

He also elaborates each one of these,

a)   Responsibility: People may feel responsible if they have the following pre requisites:

- Are aware and agree to the goals.

- Have responsibilities which have been communicated with clarity.

- Believe that they can help achieve the goals by putting their effort

Responsibilities have to be accepted by everyone in the organization to drive towards a common goal. The responsibilities across hierarchies have to be given and taken. In an organization there are possibly no individuals, so employees should take responsibilities for more than oneself. Accepting responsibilities is a choice that has been made and should feel committed towards it.

b)   Loyalty: The employee can show loyalty in the following ways:

- Participates in the success of the organization's success

- When the organization is under threat, one should defend the organization

- Takes pride to be part of the organization

- Find the positives of the organization and support the organization

- Put forth constructive criticisms, also keep those within the department or organization

Being loyal does not mean blind obedience; the employee's behaviour and work should be in order to promote the legitimate interests of the organization. So, it can even mean doing contrary but constructive and positive for the company. Sometimes it would mean saying 'No' when saying 'Yes' would mean more than ability and over committing. But feasible challenges should be accepted in order to grow. Loyalty also means showing true passion in the growth of the company and also matching it with personal ambitions. Sometimes, you will have to compromise a little for the welfare of the company.

c)   Initiative: Initiatives cannot happen without responsibility and loyalty, it also requires will and courage to take risks, to know and accept goals, coordinating with the initiatives of the colleagues, agreed communication channels, acceptance of creative mistakes, use reasoning rather than follow rules and develop own competencies.

4.3.   **Reduce differences with the parent company:** To reduce the differences between NIC and the parent Retail bank, there are decisions which need to be taken like financial decisions, production and marketing decisions, employment and personal decisions and Research and development and technology decisions. It has to be decided what are the ones that need to be centralised and what are the decisions that need to be decentralised. Some decisions have to be taken by the participation of both NIC and the parent company.

4.4.   **Respect for Women:** The issues like women not being respected by men and petty issues like being traditional, male dominated, hierarchical and status oriented and bullying, coercive and dominated by a cult personality can be avoided by introducing suitable reward example. For example "Most Popular Man of NIC" can be given to someone to whom most women vote every month. They should probably change the carpet to stay good with high heels in the board room. Petty issues cannot be taken light, because it might grow out of control. A healthy organization is one where issues are resolved right then.

5.   **HR STRATEGY:** The HR strategy is concerned with (Schuler and Huselid, 1997):

    a.   Identifying the human resource implications of business issues vital to the success of the organisation and

    b.   Implementing activities that can deal effectively with those implications.

The organizations have its own business issues vital to their success which includes:

    1.   Pursuing total quality

    2.   Having a greater capacity to change quickly

    3.   Improving productivity

    4.   Meeting the needs of the customers for continually giving better products at lower prices.

Along with key business issues unique to companies, these common key business issues also have HR implications. As an example, improving productivity may mean increasing the level of employee motivation and ability; having greater capacity to change may mean having employees who have a greater understanding of and dedication to the goals and directions of the company. So, these business issues have associated HR issues which are (Schuler and Huselid, 1997):

    i.   The need to align people with business.

    ii.   The need to link HR to the needs of the business.

    iii.   The need to facilitate uniform organisation operation.

    iv.   The need to reconceptualise the delivery of the HR function: partnership.

    v.   The need to reposition the HR department.

The HR strategy and its components can be represented in the form of a pyramid which is made up of vision, mission, values, objectives, strategic plan, tactical business plan, business processes and management system. This pyramid serves as a framework for action with a strategic long term perspective. Its power is based on employees who are the foundation for building all other elements of the Pyramid (Schuler and Huselid, 1997).

Figure 10.2: HR Strategy components

5.1. **HR Strategy for NIC:** A HR Strategy has to be designed for the NIC in order to shed 2500 people and close down more than 100 district sales and `claims offices. The Harvard Framework for HR Strategy can be used as a guideline for the change of Strategies, Policies and Practices.

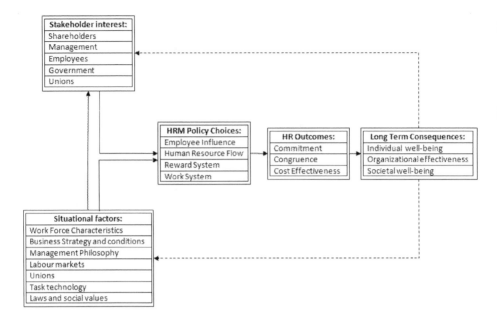

Figure 10.3: Harvard Framework for HR Strategy

5.2. **Downsizing:** When there is a crisis situation and downsizing is imminent, it is likely that the layoff will happen in a haphazard manner losing some potential employees and retaining some undeserving employees. But this is not the case in NIC; they are financially in a stable and comfortable position. So, they need to come up with a proper performance management system which addresses downsizing without downgrading (Dolan *et al,* 2000). Downsizing whatever be the situation, should be the last resort, and the following steps have to be taken (Burke and Nelson, 1997):

1) Initiation (planning revitalization efforts): It is possible to downsize without layoffs (US Department of Labour, 1995). NYNEX, the regional telephone company in New England, needed to reduce its workforce of 35,000 by 8,000 employees. By negotiating an innovative agreement with the union, NYNEX was able to downsize through early retirements, voluntary severance, job sharing, and training initiatives. Intel has avoided layoffs by using a redeployment policy that includes training to help workers find new

jobs in-house. Employee development centres offer self-assessment, career counselling, and job listings. A centralized system tracks and reports all redeployment activities (US Department of Labour, 1995). The revitalization should be a continuous improvement process irrespective of the situation of the organization.

2) Implementation (smoothing the transition): Burke and Nelson (1997) cite Leana and Feldman (1992) who proposed five issues that managers must address in the implementation of a layoff.

    i.   Explain with detail the criteria for layoff.

    ii.   The role of performance evaluations in the layoff process should be clarified by the managers.

    iii.   Treat employees who are to be laid off with respect and dignity.

    iv.   Fair recommendations have to be provided by the managers to the future employers.

    v.   The survivors after the layoff should be given social support and reassurance to boost their morale.

3) Institutionalising (healing and refocusing): Even a planned restructuring may fall short of its anticipated results. So, we need to assess the aftermath of downsizing both in terms of quantitative measures and qualitative measures. Some areas that need to be assessed include:

- Is the position of the organization competitive enough?

- Are decisions made are timely and the levels of decision making reduced?

- Have the responsibilities distributed appropriately?

- Have the processes changed to reduce cost and time and add more value to the customer.

- What is the effect on the quality and volume of output?

- How has the morale of the survivors affected?

- What is the effect on the return of the investment for the stake holders?

- Are the communication channels effective enough?

- What is the reaction of the stakeholders?

- How effective were the outplacement and assistance programs that were introduced?

To cut down the district sales and claims offices the following criteria can be used:

- The offices which are less profitable.

- The area of offices where the competitors are more popular and more profitable. Those office employees can be transferred to the areas where competitors are still struggling and can be taken advantage of.

- The employees who are not working effective enough and indulge in irresponsible manner.

The NIC are thinking of redeploying some of the employees in the call centres, which is a very positive aspect of this downsizing.

6. **CONCLUSION:** To come up with a HR Strategy in order to downsize is not a big task, any qualified manager with little assistance can do it. But it is not like dealing with machines where you just get rid of worn out machines. Here humans are involved whose future is on stake, how much of humanity can be applied and how transition is effected gracefully requires a lot of humane attitude from the Managers. The welfare of the organization should be considered with humanity with regard to both long term and short term organizational strategies to be successful and to sustain success.

REFERENCES

Bova B., Kroth M. (2001). Workplace learning and Generation X. *Journal of Workplace Learning.* 13(2), 57-65. *[Available for Athens Users at]* http://www.emeraldinsight.com/Insight/ViewContentServlet?File name=Published/EmeraldFullTextArticle/Articles/0860130202.html [Accessed on 9th May 2008]

Burke R. J., Nelson D.L., (1997). Downsizing and restructuring: lessons from the firing line for revitalizing organizations. *Leadership & Organization Development Journal.* 18(7), 324-334. *[Available for Athens Users at]* http://www.emeraldinsight.com/Insight/ViewContentServlet ?Filename=Published/EmeraldFullTextArticle/Articles/0220180701. html [Accessed on 9th May 2008]

Dolan S., Belout A., Balkin D. B. (2000). Downsizing without downgrading: learning how firms manage their survivors. *International Journal of Manpower.* 21(1), 34-47. *[Available for Athens Users at]* http://www.emeraldinsight.com/ Insight/ViewContentServlet?Filename=Published/EmeraldFullTextArticle/ Articles/0160210103.html [Accessed on 9th May 2008]

Hogan C. (2000). *Facilitating Empowerment – A Handbook for facilitators, Trainers & Individuals.* Kogan Page: London. Pg. 12-16

Møller C., (1994). Employeeship: The Necessary Prerequisite for Empowerment. *Empowerment in Organizations.* 2(2) 4-13. *[Available for Athens Users at]* http://www.emeraldinsight.com/Insight/Vie wContentServlet?Filename=Published/EmeraldFullTextArticle/ Articles/1180020201.html [Accessed on 9th May 2008]

Schuler R., Huselid M. (1997). HR Strategy in United States – examples of key issues identification and execution. *In :* Tyson S. (1997). *The Practice of Human Resource Strategy.* London: Pitman Publishing.

Self R. D. (2007). Organizational change – overcoming resistance by creating readiness. *Development and Learning in Organizations.* 21(5), 11-13. *[Available for Athens Users at]* http://www.emeraldinsight.com/Insight/ ViewContentServlet?Filename=Published/EmeraldFullTextArticle/ Articles/0810210503.html [Accessed on 9th May 2008]

ACCOUNTING AND FINANCE

CHAPTER – XI

CORPORATE FINANCE – BUSINESS REPORT
I. INTRODUCTION

The Young's Brewery wanted to do an image makeover in order to overcome the sad demise of Mr. James Young. Though John Young retired in March 2006, he had worked for 30 years in the Young's and had been on the board since 1984 and deputy Chairman since 1989. As production director, James played a key role in the many awards Young's received over the years for the quality and originality of its beers. Before retiring, he was involved in the smooth transfer of Young's brewing activities from Wandsworth to Wells & Young's. Now after the demise of Mr. James Young the company needs a publicity stunt to make a positive impact on the stakeholders, share holders and the general public. For this, the company could acquire some companies whose business is related to Young's. The Directors have proposed that they don't want anything too big, controversial or difficult to manage.

II. INVESTMENT PARAMETERS

When Young's review investment opportunities they should be looking for businesses which possess the following characteristics:

1. A strong management team with the breadth of skills and ability to grow the company quickly. Not all of the elements of the team need to be in place at the time of investment. Young's can help build the team as required.
2. Related to breweries.
3. The Company which is not a family owned is given higher priority.
4. A focus on under-served, growing and potentially substantial markets with international potential in breweries. A scaleable business model.
5. Market-driven rather than technology-led development.

6. Potential to achieve an exit for investors within four to six years.
7. The company has some scope and ideas for Young & Co to expand.
8. The company should be an UK company, listed in London Stock Exchange. However having subsidiaries in other geographical locations is an added advantage.
9. The Market Capital of the company to be acquired should be between 50 million pounds to 100 million pounds. Exceptions can be made only when the advantages are more.
10. The company should be part of FTSE 100 or FTSE AIM (Alternate Investment Market).
11. The Dividend History should be positive.
12. The company should not have complicated corporate governance methods.

III. SHORT LISTED COMPANIES (As on 12-02-08)

S. No.	Short Listed Company	Market Capital	Dividend	Share Price	Special Features
1.	Carluccio's plc	74.64 m	1.6 p	141.0	Dividends encouraging
2.	Finsbury Fd	39.32 m	1.5 p	73.5	Expand the food served to be healthy.
3.	Luminar plc	220.48 m	17.20 p	352.2	The events venues held by Luminar plc can be used by Young's to sell their products.
4.	Nichols plc	81.7 m	9.40 p	222.5	Basically a soft drink company with attractive dividend in spite of not so positive profits.
5.	Thorntons	95.66 m	4.85 p	140.0	The company is involved in manufacturing, retailing and distribution of confectionery and other sweet foods.

IV. DETAILED ANALYSIS

1. <u>CARLUCCIO'S PLC</u>

   Carluccio's Plc is engaged in the operation of Italian cafe and food shops, and retailing Italian foods. As of September 23, 2007, the Company had 34 stores. The Company offers products, such as anchovy fillets, carnaroli rice and affogato. It also runs a chain of coffee and espresso bars under the name Barista. The Company opened six Carluccio's in The Brunswick, London WC1 in October 2006; Spitalfields in London E1 in December 2006; The Trafford Centre in Manchester in March 2007; Walton in Surrey in May 2007; a concession in Bentalls, Kingston upon Thames in June 2007, and a flagship store in Covent Garden, London WC2 in August 2007.

1.1. Ratio Analysis

   The ratio analysis (including the Investment Ratios) of the Carluccio's plc is attached in APPENDIX – III.

1.2. Reasons for selecting target Company

   a. The Group was a family owned plc, but now, the family presence is almost negligible.

   b. Though it is not exactly related to pubs, Young's can collaborate with this Italian restaurant and add some special menu to their merchandise and also make the Carluccio's to sell their brands.

   c. It is a UK company listed in London Stock Exchange and does not yet have any business outside UK. In fact they are based in London and slowly moving to places around London.

   d. The company has a market capital at around 75 million pounds which is lesser than that of Young's, and hence Young's will have a good say in the company.

   e. The company is listed in the FTSE-100.

    f.   The company's management structure looks ambitious as they acquire new small companies and show promising profits.

    g.   The Annual report states the regional divisions of Italy and details the specialties of each region. This explanation is attractive and informative.

1.3.   Market profile

The Chairman cites in the Annual Report, "Mintel forecasts that the eating out market will continue growing at 6% p.a. until at least 2012."

1.4.   Industry business and prospectus

The Chairman about their performance with regard to the industry states, "Our cash returns are industry-leading and our strong cash generation has enabled us to increase our dividend payout by 47%," which is promising.

1.5.   Financial performance of the last three year

    a.   The company has an increased gross profit margin **(2005: 20.3, 2006: 19.6, 2007: 20.9).**

    b.   The net profit margin has decreased slightly.

    c.   The gearing for the company has traditionally been 0.

1.6.   Stock market analysis

    a.   More than 60% of the company's shares are held by outsiders, which is substantial and also shows that the company is not worried about outsiders' stake.

    b.   The share price is nominal 145.5 (as on 12-02-08).

    c.   They have started giving dividends since 2006, at nominal 1.6 p.

1.7.   Growth opportunity

The company has shown substantial growth financially and one would foresee that it will continue its aggressive growth.

1.8.   Geographical location
The business is mainly in UK and based in London. They are happy with their geographical spread.

2.   <u>FINSBURY FOOD GROUP:</u>
Finsbury Food Group plc is a manufacturer of celebration cakes, low-fat cake slices, and specialty, organic and gluten free breads. In October 2007, the Company acquired Anthony Alan Foods Ltd, a supplier of low-fat cakes. Finsbury Food Group produces approximately 60% of the Anthony Alan Foods product range. Anthony Alan Foods is a sales and marketing business, which under license from Weight Watchers, has the rights to distribute ambient cakes using the Weight Watchers brand in the United Kingdom and Ireland. On February 23, 2007, the Company acquired Lightbody Group Limited.

2.1.   Ratio Analysis
The ratio analysis (including the Investment Ratios) of the Finsbury Food Group plc is attached in APPENDIX – IV.

2.2.   Reasons for selecting target Company
   a. The Group is not a family owned plc, which makes it a potential plc for the Investment for the Young's.
   b. Though it is not exactly related to pubs, Young's can learn their food business and put them in place in their pubs.
   c. It is a UK company listed in London Stock Exchange having business in other countries of Europe as well.
   d. The company has a market capital at around 40 million pounds which is lesser than that of Young's, and hence Young's will have a good say in the company.
   e. The company is listed in the FTSE-AIM.
   f. The company's management structure looks ambitious as they acquire new small companies and show promising profits.

2.3.   Market profile
In the Annual report the Chief Executive talks about the market as, "It has not been the easiest of years for the bakery sector with rising input costs and the challenge of passing these costs on to customers. In the bakery markets, in which we operate, we have seen a number of business failures and it can be expected that there may be more."

2.4.   Industry business and prospectus
As always the industry is competitive, Annual report states that because of the acquisition of the "Lightbody Group Ltd," the company has moved to the second position in the cake industry.

2.5.   Financial performance of the last three year
   a.   The company has a good gross profit margin **(2005: 37.5, 2006: 39.8, 2007: 39.1)**.
   b.   The company is in need of liquid assets. The liquid ratio is low **(2005: 1.0, 2006: 0.7, 2007: 0.6)**
   c.   Their gearing ratio is high **(2005: 30.44, 2006: 121.76, 2007: 66.27)**. Young's can take advantage of their money deficit and get mutually benefited.

2.6.   Stock market analysis
   a.   The company looks like it is very liberal in issuing new shares. For example during the year to 30th June 2007, the Group issued 22.5 million new ordinary shares.
   b.   Their share price is nominal 73.5p (as on 12-02-08), but their earnings per share is low because of issuing of new shares. One would hope that in course of time when the liquidity increases, they would want to buy

back their shares and hence it is a convenient time for Young's to exit.

c. The dividend is 1.5 p which is appropriate for their small market capital.

2.7. Growth opportunity

The plc has shown considerable growth and the annual report states the reasons for the growth to be:

a. The excellent innovation work that their product development Team have put in creating new premium ranges for our customers; and the ability of the team to service seven major multiple grocers, day in day out, and to continually offer each of these customers

b. Differentiated products which reflect their individual consumer base.

If they continue the good work, they can grow within UK and also beyond into the Europe market.

2.8. Geographical location

The business is mainly in UK and has a small presence in Europe and they hope to grow geographically.

3. LUMINAR GROUP HOLDINGS PLC:

Leader in late night entertainment,. Luminar Group Holdings Plc., formerly Luminar plc, is engaged in the ownership, development and operation of nightclubs and themed bars. The Company's brands include Oceana, Liquid, Lava & Ignite, Life and The Jam House. Oceana has five bars and combines two clubs in one venue. Oceana has seven themed destinations, including a futuristic Tokyo Vodka Bar, a 1970's New York disco and a Parisian boudoir.

The Liquid brand has a contemporary design. Lava & Ignite has a classic two-room format. The main room includes sound and laser technology, and can be transformed into a venue for corporate events, live music and televised sporting events. The second room focuses on different music genres and promoters. Life caters for meetings and corporate events, as well as the traditional pub and club market. The Jam House specializes in live music. In January 19, 2007, Luminar completed the disposal of its Entertainment Division.

3.1.   Ratio Analysis
        The ratio analysis (including the Investment Ratios) of the Luminar plc is attached in APPENDIX – V.

3.2.   Reasons for selecting target Company
        a. The Group is not a family owned plc anymore, which makes it a potential plc for the Investment for the Young's.
        b. It is related to the pub business; Young's can collaborate with them and use their events venues to sell their products.
        c. It is a UK company listed in London Stock Exchange having business only in UK.
        d. The company has a market capital at around 220 million pounds which is only slightly lesser than that of Young's, still Young's might have a good say in the company because of their experience.
        e. The company is listed in the FTSE-100.
        f. The Young & Co can use the events venues for selling exclusively their products.

3.3.   Market profile
        The Luminar plc is already a leader in night club industry. In the Annual Report Alan Jackson (Chairman) says "… we can focus on the content of our units, which will drive growth and maintain our market leadership".

3.4.   Industry business and prospectus

The industrial leadership is embedded in their one of the mission statement itself, "To achieve the highest standard of customer service and entertainment in the leisure industry by offering value for money within our venues".

3.5.   Financial performance of the last three year
   a. The company has a good gross profit margin (**2005: 51.4, 2006: 52.0, 2007:53.7**)
   b. The Current Ratio (Acid Test Ratio) is significant (**2005: 82.7, 2006: 83.7, 2007: 84.4**).
   c. The gearing has been decreasing and liquid assets are substantial. That shows how much the UK youth spends or wastes??

3.6.   Stock market analysis
   a. More than 38% of the company's shares are owned by outsiders and hence they are not scared about letting others in.
   b. Their share price is nominal 356 (as on 12-02-08), and the dividend is a generous 17.2 p.

3.7.   Growth opportunity

The Luminar plc right now focuses only on customers of age group 18-30, this can be changed by organizing events especially for other age group of people.

3.8.   Geographical location

The Group has only one geographic segment, being the UK, as no regions of the UK expose the Group to differentiated risks and returns.

4. <u>NICHOL'S GROUP PLC:</u>

    Nichols plc is engaged in the supply of soft drinks and other beverages to the retail, wholesale, catering, licensed and leisure industries. It comprises two operations: Soft Drinks and Dispense Systems. Soft Drinks division consists of the sale of the Vimto brand worldwide, and the Panda and Sunkist brands in the United Kingdom. The Vimto branded licensed product range includes Vimto Chewy Sweets, Vimto Tongue Ticklers, Vimto Bon-Bon Bags, Vimto Lollipops and Vimto Ice Lollies. During the year ended December 31, 2006, the Company's Panda brand range of soft drinks was completely re-formulated and then re-launched as a natural flavoured, sugar free soft drink aimed at the children's soft drink market in the United Kingdom. Dispense Systems operation consists of cabana and Beacon businesses and is focused on dispensing cold soft drinks on draught. On January 12, 2006, the Company disposed of its Beacon Trading Limited, which was engaged in hot beverages business.

4.1. Ratio Analysis

       The ratio analysis (including the Investment Ratios) of the Nichol's plc is attached in APPENDIX – VI.

4.2. Reasons for selecting target Company
       a. The Group is family owned plc, but they do not deny the entry of outsiders, about 33% of their shares are held by outsiders.
       b. It is related to pubs, Young's can collaborate with them and share their technical knowledge and develop hybrid products (a combination of soft and hard drink).
       c. It is a UK company listed in London Stock Exchange having business in other countries of as well.
       d. The company has a market capital at around 35 million

pounds which is lesser than that of Young's, and hence Young's will have a good say in the company.

e. The company is listed in the FTSE-100.

f. Soft drinks sales are seasonal depending on the climate, but still Nichol's brand Vimto is well known so that can be exploited by the aggressive marketing of Young's and get mutually benefited. Basically to learn their marketing for the Young's.

4.3. Market profile

In the Annual Report John Nichols (Chairman) talks about the market, "Despite the highly competitive nature of the markets in which we operate, we will continue to pursue our strategy of vigorously marketing the Vimto brand to drive volume growth and maintain margin."

4.4. Industry business and prospectus

The industry is competitive with very big established players and also has scope for growth.

4.5. Financial performance of the last three year

    a. The company has a good gross profit margin **(2005: 41.0, 2006: 52.3, 2007: 52.6)**

    b. The Current Ratio (Acid Test Ratio) is enormous **(2004: 191.4, 2005: 105.9, 2006:245.3)**.

    c. They got rid of their loans; hence their gearing is reduced to zero **(2004: 36.98, 2005: 84.25, 2006: 0.00)**.

4.6. Stock market analysis

    a. More than 31% of the company's shares are owned by outsiders and hence they are not scared about letting others in.

       b. Their share price is nominal 245.5 (as on 12-02-08), and the dividend is an ample 6.50p.

4.7.   Growth opportunity

The plc has presence in 65 countries all around the world and geared to grow more which is visible in their introduction of new products.

4.8.   Geographical location

The business operates not only in UK, but also in Middle East, Africa, Rest of the world.

5.   <u>THORNTONS PLC:</u> Thorntons PLC is principally engaged in the manufacturing, retailing and distribution of confectionery and other sweet foods. Its subsidiaries include Strand Court Properties Limited, Thorntons (Jersey) Limited and Thorntons Card Services Limited. During the fiscal year ended June 30, 2007 (fiscal 2007), it opened 23 new franchise stores and closed 17. As of fiscal 2007, the Company had 368 stores and 218 franchise stores.

5.1.   Ratio Analysis

The ratio analysis (including the Investment Ratios) of the Thornton's plc is attached in APPENDIX – VII.

5.2.   Reasons for selecting target Company

       a. The Group is not a family owned plc, which makes it a potential plc for the Investment for the Young's.

       b. Though it is not exactly related to pubs, Young's can collaborate with them and create products of chocolate and champagne for seasonal markets.

       c. It is a UK company listed in London Stock Exchange having business in other countries of Europe as well.

       d. The company has a market capital at around 95 million

pounds which is lesser than that of Young's, and hence Young's will have a good say in the company.

e. The company is listed in the FTSE-100.

f. The confectionery business has a special appeal during seasonal festivals which does not mean it sells only during seasons; it is good in non-seasons and better in seasons.

5.3.   Market profile

In the Annual Report Mark R Henson (Company Secretary) talks about the market, "We operate in a very competitive market. The UK confectionery market has many strong players and the recent slowdown in consumer spending has intensified competition. Product innovation is the key to combating and overcoming the competition. The Company has a rigorous process for identifying, researching and developing new product ideas, which is regularly reviewed and improved. The Company's evolving multi-channel strategy is also a means by which it can satisfy consumers' needs better than the competition."

5.4.   Industry business and prospectus

The confectionery industry is competitive and also has scope for growth.

5.5.   Financial performance of the last three year

a. The company has a good gross profit margin (**2005: 51.4, 2006: 52.0, 2007:53.7**)

b. The Current Ratio (Acid Test Ratio) is substantial (**2005: 76.4, 2006: 111.0, 2007: 76.5**).

c. They got rid of their long term loans; hence their gearing is reduced in the last couple of years (**2005: 92.68, 2006: 52.98, 2007: 54.46**).

5.6.   Stock market analysis

a.   More than 55% of the company's shares are owned by outsiders and hence they are not scared about letting others in.

b.   Their share price is nominal 140 (as on 12-02-08), and the dividend is an ample 4.85p.

5.7.   Growth opportunity

The chairman states that, "…our investments in the improvement of our stores, an emphasis on developing innovative and exciting products and the support of more imaginative marketing activities. We will remain focused on improving our customer offer by maintaining our commitment towards expanding our store portfolio and franchise partners and enlarging our commercial and website customer base, all of which will provide a solid platform on which to present occur continually evolving range of quality chocolates and confectionery." This statement assures positive growth in future as well.

5.8.   Geographical location

The business operates only in UK and hence it is simple to manage without the problems of foreign exchanges and ever fluctuating currencies.

V. PRO FORMA BALANCE SHEET:

The Fixed Assets are revalued according the rates as on 2007 (previously it was 1997) and it is assumed that it will increase the total asset by 200 million pounds. Also the deal of investing would cost them 50 million pounds. One would suggest that they take a bank loan. The interim report says that the debts of Young & Co at the end of the interim period are £94.5 million. Once adjusted for the remaining £58.7 million due from Minerva in January, this leaves an adjusted net debt position of £35.8 million which is not a threatening debt figure.

The extrapolated Pro Forma balance sheet is attached in (APPENDIX – VIII).

VI. INVESTMENT PORTFOLIO:

It is suggested that Young's invest 10 million each in 5 companies. Depending on the market capital of the target company, the shareholdings for Young & Co in the target company is shown below:

Amount invested (m)	Company	Share price in (p)	Total No. of shares	% holdings
10	Carluccio's plc	141.0	56924000	12.46%
10	Finsbury Food Group	73.5	33286620	24.47%
10	Luminar plc	352.2	70.6 million	4.02%
10	Nichols plc	222.5	36685868	12.25%
10	Thornton's	140.0	66346144	10.77%

VII. REJECTED COMPANIES

The following are the companies which were under consideration and rejected because of specific reasons given below:

S. No.	Name of the company	Reasons for rejection
1.	Blavod plc	Too small and owner unclear
2.	AG Barr plc	Too big, market capital more than 200 million and did not select it because we had already selected Nichol's which is a worthy investment target.
3.	Diageo plc	Too big, has a Market Capital of 27.3 billion, Young's is too small when compared to this.
4.	Garner plc	Too small, Market Capital of 1.71 m, it is way small when compared to the Young's
5.	SAB Miller plc	Too big, Market Capital of 17.33 billion.
6.	Zetar plc	No dividend history. It is an investment company which does not match with our criteria
7.	Wynnstay Property Group	It has a market capital at around 14 million which is relatively small.
8.	Oakdene plc	It has a market capital at around 18.3 million which is relatively small.
9.	Telford HMS	It has a market capital at around 79.77 million which is involved in acquisition and development of properties which is not related to the Young's
10.	Celtic plc	It has business football clubs which the Young's might not be interested at this point of time.
11.	Clapham House	The Dividend History is not good, they have not yet started to give dividends.
12.	Pubs N Bars	Very small company relatively, with Market Capital of 9.24 m.
13.	Georgica plc	Running in loss, verge of bankruptcy.
14.	Enterprise Inns	The Market Capital is 2.16 bn which is huge.
15.	Whitbread	The Market Capital is 2.20 bn which is enormous.

VIII. CONCLUSION

There are companies which lost everything they had because of wrong investment decisions and there are companies which changed their whole business outlook successfully because of wise investment and merger/acquisition decisions. At this juncture, we suggest Young's to give their decision an honest look and evaluate their decisions genuinely and also reckon the risks they will have to face because of this investment decision. But business is all about taking wise risks at the appropriate time. And without risks they will reach nowhere in this competitive world. They should weigh this juncture with both the positives and negatives.

And finally, we wish them "All the Best" in their endeavours.

LEADERSHIP

CHAPTER - XII

FUTURE LEADERS

The recent concepts of emotional intelligence and Spiritual growth have gained momentum and might be the key for the future leaders. But let's see the hidden potential competencies. In the recent trends the future leader is expected to 1. Exhibit feminine qualities irrespective of the gender of the leader, 2. Face reality head on and 3. Work in a virtual environment. Let's see these competencies one by one.

Ford (2005) says that "feminine qualities such as empathy, capacity for listening, relational skills etc." needs to be part of a leader irrespective of gender. Empathy is defined as, "The ability to recognise and understand the emotional makeup of others; skill in dealing with the emotional responses of others." According to Appelbaum and Shakiro (1993), the following characteristics of women stand out:

1. Women's emphasis on assisting others to achieve the other's goals

2. The emphasis on establishing the security of intimate relationships prior to consideration of personal achievement.

3. Women's tendency to define themselves in relation to others.

4. Women's inclination towards self-disclosure and the development of close relationships with others.

They conclude that "There are certain masculine and feminine characteristics that have a positive impact on leadership effectiveness and it is possible for both men and women to exhibit both types of characteristics."

The next competency is "to face reality head on". Heifetz, 1999, in one of his interviews to Taylor, about future leaders says that, "The real heroism of leadership involves having the courage to face reality -- and helping the people around you to face reality.... It is to mobilizing people to tackle tough challenges -- is what defines the new job of the leader." He also says that an effective leader is one who prioritizes based on reality about what's essential and what's not. He advises that, "Leaders of the future need to have the stomach for conflict and uncertainty -- among their people and within themselves. That's why leaders of the future need to have an experimental mind-set. Some decisions will work, some won't. Some projects will pay off, some won't. But every decision and every project will teach you and your organization something about how the world is changing -- and about how your company compares with its competition."

Virtual Leadership is the next chosen future competency of a leader. Oertig and Buergi (2006) say that "Globalization has led to many changes in the nature of project team work. Many international companies have projects spanning a variety of nationalities, involving great geographical distance and a range of time zones .... (In such a scenario) ... The factors to which particular attention should be given include the following:

1. The importance of selecting creative leaders with a collaborative leadership style and excellent communication skills. Leaders in a matrix organization must be able to lead by influence rather than authority, managing personality issues as well as the functional and cultural mindsets of team members. At the same time they need to keep finding new ways to communicate across time zones and work round geographical barriers.

2. The need for top management to continue to facilitate face-to-face communication and relationship building. The trend towards ever-increasing use of technology can be efficient and clearly saves costs, but has its price. This study shows the importance of continuing to meet face to face in the technological age to help promote the development of swift trust (Oertig and Buergi, 2006 cite Meyerson et al., 1996) among team members.

3. The value of ongoing investment in language and intercultural communication training. Training is particularly important for new members of project teams working on different continents, to help reduce potential distrust, and allow teams to gel more quickly and work together efficiently."

Conclusion

"[There are] almost as many definitions of leadership as there are persons who have attempted to define the concept," (Horner, 1997 cites Stogdill, 1974)

Researching about leadership is like a voyage in a perilous and uncharted sea. We have just attempted in trying to find the direction. It is considered that "the study of leadership in an organization is a field in flux, with many cherished assumptions, theories and methodological proclivities under siege", (Bryman, 1986). That sums up everything about leadership. I would like to conclude with Jesus' words adapted as, "With professionalism, treat your sub-ordinates the way you like to be treated by your bosses".

Act Humanely! Act responsibly!

References:

1. Appelbaum, Stephen H, Shapiro, Barbara T , (1993), "Why can't men lead like women?" *Leadership & Organization Development Journal* Vol. 14, Iss. 7, pg. 28, 7 pgs. Retrieved from World Wide Web on 19th Nov 2007

http://proquest.umi.com/pqdlink?Ver=1&Exp=11-17-2012&FMT=7&DID=81757&RQT=309&clientId=28275

2. Bryman, Alan, (1986), *"Leadership and Organizations"*, Oxon: Routeledge & Kegan Paul Plc. Pg. 199

3. Chapman, Alan, (2006), *"Action centred Leadership"*, Retrieved from World Wide Web on 18th Nov 2007, http://www.businessballs.com/action.htm

4. Dovey, Ken, Singhota, Jai, (2005), "Learning and knowing in teams: Lessons for business from professional sport", *Development and Learning in Organizations: An International Journal* vol:19 iss:3 pg:18-20. Retrieved from World Wide Web on 19th Nov 2007 http://www.emeraldinsight.com/Insight/viewPDF.jsp?Filename=html/Output/Published/EmeraldFullTextArticle/Pdf/0810190305.pdf

5. Ford, Jackie (2005) "Examining leadership through critical feminist readings", *Journal of health organization and management* vol:19 iss:3 pg:236 -251 Retrieved from World Wide Web on 19th Nov 2007 at http://www.emeraldinsight.com/Insight/viewPDF.jsp?Filename=html/Output/Published/EmeraldFullTextArticle/Pdf/0250190305.pdf

6. Kilpatrick, Andrea and Silverman, Les, (2005), "The power of vision", *STRATEGY & LEADERSHIP* 33(2) 25-26. Retrieved from World Wide Web on 19th Nov 2007 http://www.emeraldinsight.com/Insight/viewPDF.jsp?Filename=html/Output/Published/EmeraldFullTextArticle/Pdf/2610330204.pdf

7. Liu, Jonathan, Srivastava, Ashok, Woo, Hong Seng (1998), "Transference of skills between sports and business", *Source: Journal of European Industrial Training*, vol:22 iss:3 pg:93 -112. Retrieved from World Wide Web on 19th Nov 2007 http://www.emeraldinsight.com/Insight/viewPDF.jsp?Filename=html/Output/Published/EmeraldFullTextArticle/Pdf/0030220301.pdf

8. Morden, Tony, (1997), "Leadership as vision", *Management Decision* 35(9) 668-676 Retrieved from World Wide Web on 19th Nov 2007
   http://www.emeraldinsight.com/Insight/viewPDF.jsp?Filename=html/Output/Published/EmeraldFullTextArticle/Pdf/0010350904.pdf

9. Syrett, Michel & Hogg, Clare, (1992), *"Frontiers of Leadership – An Essential Reader",* Oxford: BlackWell Pg. 102-103

10. Taylor, Bernard (2003), "Board leadership: balancing entrepreneurship and strategy with accountability and control", *Corporate governance the international journal for effective board performance* vol:3 iss:2 pg:3 -5 Retrieved from World Wide Web on 19th Nov 2007
   http://www.emeraldinsight.com/Insight/viewPDF.jsp?Filename=html/Output/Published/EmeraldFullTextArticle/Pdf/2680030201.pdf

11. Taylor, William C. (1999) "The Leader of the Future - Harvard's Ronald Heifetz offers a short course on the future of leadership." Retrieved from World Wide Web on 19th Nov 2007 http://www.fastcompany.com/magazine/25/heifetz.html

APPENDIX – I

The features of the different generations of iPod and iPod mini

iPod Type/Features	1G iPod	2G iPod	3G iPod	4G iPod	iPod mini
Fire Wire Port		X	X/*	X/*	X/*
Head Phone Port	X	X	X	X	X
Hold Switch	X	X	X	X	X
Scroll Wheel	X				
Touch Wheel		X	X		
Touch/Click Wheel				X	X

* -- All the 3G iPods, 4G iPods and iPod mini have a Fire Wire/Dock Connector on the bottom of the Unit.

APPENDIX – II

The price of McDonald's Big Mac in various countries is put for comparison.

Country	Price of Big Mac	Cost in UK £
Australia	$2.65	0.87
South Africa	R7.80	0.92
USA	$1.89	1.13
Korea	2,600won	1.13
India	Rs80	1.19
New Zealand	$3.65	1.20
Turkey	500,000TL	1.25
Japan	280yen	1.27
Spain	375psts	1.44
Brazil	2.95reals	1.52
Ireland	IERP1.85	1.52
Switzerland	SF4.02	1.58
Germany	DM4.90	1.58
Italy	L4,800	1.59
Austria	Sch34	1.61
Belgium	BF105	1.66
Denmark	DKK19.95	1.80
UK	£1.81	1.81

APPENDIX – III

Ratio Analysis for Carluccio's plc

(The annual reports for the companies were obtained and are available in http://www.northcote.co.uk/)

Name of the company	Carlucious plc		
Balance Sheet Analysis Spread Sheet	2005	2006	2007
Date of auditors certificate			
(State if qualified)	n/q	n/q	n/q
Currency (in £)	£000's	£000's	£000's
QUICK ASSETS			
Cash & Bank	2,038.00	2,642.00	3,145.00
Short-term investments and deposits			
Debtors/Accounts Receivable/Bills Receivable	1,398.00	1,643.00	1,925.00
TOTAL QUICK ASSETS	**3,436.00**	**4,285.00**	**5,070.00**
Stock - Finished Goods	4,376.00	979.00	1,068.00
- Work in Progress			
- Raw Materials	215.00	244.00	313.00
	8,027.00	**5,508.00**	**6,451.00**
CURRENT LIABILITIES			
Creditors/Accounts Payable/Bills Payable	2,811.00	3,117.00	3,803.00
Hire Purchase/Leasing - less than one year			
Current Portion Long Term Debt			
Provisions for liabilities			
Due to Group Companies			
Due to Directors			
Dividends			
Taxation - PAYE, NI, VAT etc.	928.00	1,416.00	1,535.00

Corporation Tax	411.00	178.00	649.00
Accruals and deferred income	3,169.00	4,004.00	4,564.00
Other Current Liabilities			
TOTAL CURRENT LIABILITIES	**7,319.00**	**8,715.00**	**10,551.00**
LIQUID SURPLUS/(DEFICIT)	**-2,943.00**	**-3,207.00**	**-4,100.00**
QUICK ASSET SURPLUS/ (DEFICIT)	**10,860.00**	**-2,940.00**	**10,860.00**
FIXED AND OTHER ASSETS			
Lease hold Improvements	7,603.00	9,929.00	12,919.00
Leasehold Properties	2,056.00	2,492.00	2,721.00
Equipment, fittings & vehicles	2,568.00	3,208.00	4,057.00
Assets in the course of construction	316.00	381.00	374.00
Associates			
Others Unlisted investments			
Due from Group Companies			
Goodwill	24.00	22.00	20.00
TOTAL FIXED AND OTHER ASSETS	**12,567.00**	**16,032.00**	**20,091.00**
TERM AND OTHER LIABILITIES			
Future Taxation			
Deferred Taxation			
Hire Purchase/Leasing			
Loans Due for Repayment - one to five years			
Loans Due for Repayment beyond five years			
Pension Liability			
Provision & charges	948.00	1,290.00	1,433.00
	948.00	1,290.00	1,433.00
Minority Interests			
TOTAL TERM & OTHER LIABILITIES	**948.00**	**1,290.00**	**1,433.00**

NET TANGIBLE ASSSETS - SURPLUS/(DEFICIT)	**8,676.00**	**11,535.00**	**14,558.00**
Financed by			
Shared Capital - Issued	2,732.00	2,840.00	2,849.00
Share premium account	1,544.00	1,684.00	1,713.00
Capital Reserves			
Distributable Reserves	4,400.00	7,011.00	9,996.00
Less: (Goodwill and Intangibles)			
SHAREHOLDERS FUNDS - SURPLUS/(DEFICIT)	**8,676.00**	**11,535.00**	**14,558.00**
PROFIT SUMMARY			
Profit Before Interest and Tax	5,663.00	5,720.00	8,002.00
Profit on sale of Fixed Assets	11.00	41.00	0.00
Investment Income and Interest Receivable	38.00	39.00	100.00
Profit Before Interest Paid	**5,712.00**	**5,800.00**	**8,102.00**
(Interest Paid)	-58.00	-18.00	-26.00
Profit Before Tax(PBT)	**5,654.00**	**5,782.00**	**8,076.00**
(Taxation)	-897.00	-687.00	-806.00
(Minority Interests)			
Extraordinary items			
Attributable Profit/Loss After Tax (APAT)	**4,757.00**	**5,095.00**	**7,270.00**
(Dividends)	-316.00	0.00	-1,194.00
Residual Profit/Loss	**4,441.00**	**5,095.00**	**6,076.00**
Additional Capital and Reserve Movements			
Revaluation			
Exchange Losses			
Goodwill W/O			
NET VARIATION IN SURPLUS/ (DEFICIT)	**4,441.00**	**5,095.00**	**6,076.00**
KEY FIGURES AND RATIOS			

Sales	36,844.00	45,759.00	53,979.00
Cost of Goods Sold	29,367.00	36,810.00	42,685.00
Gross Profit	7,477.00	8,949.00	11,294.00
Depreciation			
Capital Employed	8,676.00	11,535.00	14,558.00
PROFITABILITY			
Gross Profit Margin			
(Gross Profit ÷Sales x100)	20.3	19.6	20.9
Net Profit Margin			
(Residual profit ÷ Sales x 100)	12.1	11.1	11.3
Return on Capital Employed			
(Profit Before Interest & Tax ÷	65.3	49.6	55.0
Capital Employed) x 100)			
CONTROL/LIQUIDITY			
Credit Given			
(Debtors ÷ Sales x 360)	14	13	13
Credit Taken			
(Creditors ÷ Cost of Goods Sold x 360)	34	30	32
Stock Turnover			
(Stock÷ Cost of Goods Sold x 360)	56	12	12
Current Ratio			
(Current Assets ÷ Current Liabilities) x 100	109.7	63.2	61.1
Liquid Ratio			
(Quick Assets ÷ Current Liabilities) x 100	46.9	49.2	48.1
GEARING AND SOLVENCY			
Gross Gearing			
*(Total Borrowings ÷ Surplus)*100*	0.00	0.00	0.00
INVESTMENT RATIOS			
Profit after Tax	2222	2380	3847
Preference Dividend (if any)			

Number of Ordinary Shares in Issue	52409	56300	56924
Earnings per share in pence ('p')	**4.24**	**4.23**	**6.76**
(Profit after Tax & Preference Dividend (if any) ÷			
Number of Ordinary Shares in Issue)			
Market Price per share as on (29-01-08)	141	141	141
Price / Earnings Ratio	**33.26**	**33.35**	**20.86**
(Market Price per share ÷ Earnings per Share)			
Dividend per Share	0	1.5	1.60
Dividend Yield	**0.00**	**1.06**	**1.13**
(Dividend per Share ÷ Market Price per Share x 100)			
Dividend Cover		**2.82**	**4.22**
(Earnings per Share ÷ Dividend per Share			
Shareholders' Funds (Ord. Shared + Res + Pref. Shares - if any)		11535	14558
Return on Equity		**0.21**	**0.26**
(Profit after Tax ÷ Shareholders' Funds)			
Share % for Young's by investing 10 million			12.459066
((Amount invested/Share Price)/No. Of shares issued)*100			
Market capital			80.26284
(No. Of shares issued x Share Price)			

APPENDIX – IV

Ratio Analysis for Finsbury Food Group

(The annual reports for the companies were obtained and are available in http://www.northcote.co.uk/)

Name of the company	Finsbury Food Group		
Balance Sheet Analysis Spread Sheet	2004	2005	2006
Date of auditors certificate		22/3/2006	15/3/2007
(State if qualified)	n/q	n/q	n/q
Currency (in £)	£000's	£000's	£000's
QUICK ASSETS			
Cash & Bank	12369	8035	334
Short-term investments and deposits			
Debtors/Accounts Receivable/Bills Receivable	672	1502	3627
TOTAL QUICK ASSETS	**13041**	**9537**	**3961**
Stock - Finished Goods			
- Work in Progress	210	416	967
- Raw Materials			
TOTAL CURRENT ASSETS	**13251**	**9953**	**4928**
CURRENT LIABILITIES			
Creditors/Accounts Payable/Bills Payable	1275	1550	7960
Hire Purchase/Leasing - less than one year			
Current Portion Long Term Debt			
(Secured Debt - memo item)			
Due to Group Companies			
Due to Directors			
Dividends			
Taxation - PAYE, NI, VAT etc.	377	774	1275
Corporation Tax	59	110	26

Accruals and deferred income	795	826	2920
Other Current Liabilities	395	7178	1176
TOTAL CURRENT LIABILITIES	**2901**	**10438**	**13357**
LIQUID SURPLUS/(DEFICIT)	**10350**	**-485**	**-8429**
QUICK ASSET SURPLUS/ (DEFICIT)	**10140**	**-901**	**-9396**
FIXED AND OTHER ASSETS			
Freehold Properties	1311	946	1461
Leasehold Properties	3209	7333	21443
Equipment, fittings & vehicles	908	1402	5019
Investments - Subsidiaries			
Defined benefit pension asset			
Others Unlisted investments			
Due from Group Companies			
Goodwill	17850	14089	38130
TOTAL FIXED AND OTHER ASSETS	**23278**	**23770**	**66053**
TERM AND OTHER LIABILITIES			
Future Taxation			
Hire Purchase/Leasing			
Deferred Taxation			
Loans Due for Repayment beyond one year	12918	425	8200
Pension Liability			
Provision & charges	16	1149	61
	12934	**1574**	**8261**
Less: (Goodwill and Intangibles)			
TOTAL TERM & OTHER LIABILITIES	**12934**	**1574**	**8261**
NET TANGIBLE ASSSETS - SURPLUS/(DEFICIT)	**20694**	**21711**	**49363**
Financed by			

Redemption Reserve			
Shared Capital - Issued	19,563	19769	44061
Capital Reserves	1995	2029	3492
Minority Interests			
Distributable Reserves	-864	-87	1810
SHAREHOLDERS FUNDS - SURPLUS/(DEFICIT)	**20694**	**21711**	**49363**
PROFIT SUMMARY			
Profit Before Interest and Tax	-268	604	4958
Profit on sale of Fixed Assets			
Investment Income	668	421	-285
Interest Receivable	682	463	65
Profit Before Interest Paid	**1082**	**1488**	**4738**
(Interest Paid)	-350	-42	-350
Profit Before Tax(PBT)	**14**	**1446**	**4388**
(Taxation)	-18	-59	-84
(Minority Interests)			
Extraordinary items			
Attributable Profit/Loss After Tax (APAT)	**-4**	**1387**	**4304**
(Dividends)	0	0	0
Residual Profit/Loss	**-4**	**1387**	**4304**
Additional Capital and Reserve Movements			
Revaluation			
Exchange Losses			
Goodwill W/O			
NET VARIATION IN SURPLUS/ (DEFICIT)	**-4**	**1387**	**4304**
KEY FIGURES AND RATIOS			
Sales	4672	17332	45951

Cost of Goods Sold	3414	11459	28941
Gross Profit	1258	5873	17010
Depreciation	0	0	0
Capital Employed	20694	21711	49363
PROFITABILITY			
Gross Profit Margin			
(Gross Profit ÷Sales x100)	26.9	33.9	37.0
Net Profit Margin			
(Residual profit ÷ Sales x 100)	-0.1	8.0	9.4
Return on Capital Employed			
(Profit Before Interest & Tax ÷	-1.3	2.8	10.0
Capital Employed) x 100)			
CONTROL/LIQUIDITY			
Credit Given			
(Debtors ÷ Sales x 360)	52	31	28
Credit Taken			
(Creditors ÷ Cost of Goods Sold x 360)	134	49	99
Stock Turnover			
(Stock÷ Cost of Goods Sold x 360)	22	13	12
Current Ratio			
(Current Assets ÷ Current Liabilities)	4.6	1.0	0.4
Liquid Ratio			
(Quick Assets ÷ Current Liabilities	4.5	0.9	0.3
GEARING AND SOLVENCY			
Gross Gearing			
(Total Borrowings ÷ Surplus)*100	62.42	1.96	16.61
INVESTMENT RATIOS			
Profit after Tax	-4	1387	4304
Preference Dividend (if any)	0	0	0
Number of Ordinary Shares in Issue	19954020	20423047	33010898
Earnings per share in pence ('p')	**-0.02**	**6.79**	**13.04**

(Profit after Tax & Preference Dividend (if any) ÷			
Number of Ordinary Shares in Issue)			
Market Price per share as on (29-01-08)	202.5	202.5	202.5
Price / Earnings Ratio	**-10101.72**	**29.82**	**15.53**
(Market Price per share ÷ Earnings per Share)			
Dividend per Share	1.5	1.5	1.50
Dividend Yield	**0.74**	**0.74**	**0.74**
(Dividend per Share ÷ Market Price per Share x 100)			
Dividend Cover	**-0.01**	**4.53**	**8.69**
(Earnings per Share ÷ Dividend per Share			
Shareholders' Funds (Ord. Shared + Res + Pref. Shares - if any)	20694	21711	49363
Return on Equity	**0.00**	**0.06**	**0.09**
(Profit after Tax ÷ Shareholders' Funds)			

APPENDIX – V
Ratio Analysis for Luminar plc

(The annual reports for the companies were obtained and are available in http://www.northcote.co.uk/)

Name of the company	LUMINAR PLC		
Balance Sheet Analysis Spread Sheet	2005	2006	2007
Date of auditors certificate			
(State if qualified)	n/q	n/q	n/q
Currency (in £)	£m	£m	£m
QUICK ASSETS			
Cash & Bank	22.6	71.9	14.7
Short-term investments and deposits			
Debtors/Accounts Receivable/Bills Receivable	5.1	13	7.3
TOTAL QUICK ASSETS	**27.7**	**84.9**	**22**
Stock - Finished Goods	3	2.6	2.4
- Work in Progress			
- Raw Materials			
Assets classified as held for sale	44.6	33.4	13.6
TOTAL CURRENT ASSETS	**75.3**	**121**	**38**
CURRENT LIABILITIES			
Creditors/Accounts Payable/Bills Payable	9.5	8.8	6.6
Hire Purchase/Leasing - less than one year	0.9		
Current Portion Long Term Debt			
(Secured Debt - memo item)			
Due to Group Companies			
Due to Directors			
Social securities and other taxes	7.9	4.3	2.1
Accrual for share buy back		0	1.5
derivative financial instruments	0	0.5	0
Dividends			
Taxation - PAYE, NI, VAT etc.	11.8	30.2	35.6

Provisions	0.6	2.3	4.3
Liabilities Classified as held for sale	8.8	12.2	3.7
Corporation Tax			
Accruals	21.1	10.3	15.5
Deferred income	0.1	0.6	0.5
Other Creditors		0	1.8
TOTAL CURRENT LIABILITIES	**60.7**	**69.2**	**71.6**
LIQUID SURPLUS/(DEFICIT)	**14.6**	**51.7**	**-33.6**
QUICK ASSET SURPLUS/(DEFICIT)	**-33**	**15.7**	**-49.6**
FIXED AND OTHER ASSETS			
Freehold Properties	96	76.7	55.2
Long Leasehold Properties	9.1	0.7	0.4
Short Leasehold Properties	99.3	95.7	82.6
Equipment, fittings & vehicles	209.1	210	162.2
Trade and other receivables		0	19.5
Investments - Subsidiaries			30.3
Others noncurrent assets	7.6	7.4	4.7
Other intangible assets	1.1	2.1	1.8
Due from Group Companies			
Goodwill	203.1	178	174.9
TOTAL FIXED AND OTHER ASSETS	**625.3**	**570**	**531.6**
TERM AND OTHER LIABILITIES			
Future Taxation			
Deferred Taxation	59.1	43.9	26.9
Hire Purchase/Leasing	7.1	5.6	8
Loans Due for Repayment - one to five years			
Loans Due for Repayment beyond One year	179.1	179	72.7
Deferred income	4.4	9.3	7.2
Pension Liability			
Provision & charges	3.2	5.5	4.4
	252.9	**244**	**119.2**

TOTAL TERM & OTHER LIABILITIES	252.9	244	119.2
NET TANGIBLE ASSSETS - SURPLUS/ (DEFICIT)	387	378	378.8
Financed by			
Shared Capital - Issued	18	18.3	17.5
Share premium	60.9	60.9	61
Capital Reserves	2.3	2.3	2.3
Capital Redemption reserves		0	0.8
Merger reserve	280.2	241	235.3
equity reserve	0.3	0.5	0.4
Retained Earnings	25	55.2	61.5
SHAREHOLDERS FUNDS - SURPLUS/ (DEFICIT)	387	378	378.8
PROFIT SUMMARY			
Profit Before Interest and Tax	99.9	74.1	59.2
Profit on sale of Fixed Assets	11.4	5.2	12.1
Investment Income and Interest Receivable	1.1	2.6	1.3
Profit Before Interest Paid	**112.4**	**81.9**	**72.6**
(Interest Paid)	-14.3	-11.1	-8.4
Profit Before Tax(PBT)	**98.1**	**70.8**	**64.2**
(Taxation)	-6.8	7.1	-3.8
(Minority Interests)			
Extraordinary items			
Attributable Profit/Loss After Tax (APAT)	**91.3**	**77.9**	**60.4**
(Dividends)	-9.5	-10.3	-11.4
Residual Profit/Loss	**81.8**	**67.6**	**49**
Additional Capital and Reserve Movements			
Revaluation			
Exchange Losses			
Goodwill W/O			

NET VARIATION IN SURPLUS/ (DEFICIT)	**81.8**	**67.6**	**49**
KEY FIGURES AND RATIOS			
Sales	288.1	195	204
Cost of Goods Sold	49.7	31.7	31.9
Gross Profit	238.4	163	172.1
Depreciation			
Capital Employed	387	378	378.8
PROFITABILITY			
Gross Profit Margin			
(Gross Profit ÷Sales x100)	**82.7**	**83.7**	**84.4**
Net Profit Margin			
(Residual profit ÷ Sales x 100)	**28.4**	**34.7**	**24.0**
Return on Capital Employed			
(Profit Before Interest & Tax ÷	**25.8**	**19.6**	**15.6**
Capital Employed) x 100)			
CONTROL/LIQUIDITY			
Credit Given			
(Debtors ÷ Sales x 360)	**6**	**24**	**13**
Credit Taken			
(Creditors ÷ Cost of Goods Sold x 360)	**75**	**100**	**74**
Stock Turnover			
(Stock÷ Cost of Goods Sold x 360)	**22**	**30**	**27**
Current Ratio			
(Current Assets ÷ Current Liabilities)	**124.1**	**174.7**	**53.1**
Liquid Ratio			
(Quick Assets ÷ Current Liabilities	**45.6**	**122.7**	**30.7**
GEARING AND SOLVENCY			
Gross Gearing			
(Total Borrowings ÷ Surplus)*100	**46.28**	**47.37**	**19.19**
Net Gearing			

(Net Borrowings ÷ Surplus)			
Gearing (Total Liabilities)			
OTHER KEY FIGURES			
Capital Expenditure			
Capital Commitments: Contracted			
Authorised			
Contingent Liabilities: Guarantees			
Other			
Leasing Obligations			
Director's Remuneration			
INVESTMENT RATIOS			
Profit after Tax	17.5	11.5	14.6
Preference Dividend (if any)	9.5	10.3	11.4
Number of Ordinary Shares in Issue	73.2	73.2	70.6
Earnings per share in pence ('p')	**23.91**	**29.78**	**20.68**
(Profit after Tax & Preference Dividend (if any) ÷			
Number of Ordinary Shares in Issue)			
Market Price per share as on (29-01-08)	352.2	352	352.2
Price / Earnings Ratio	**14.73**	**11.83**	**17.03**
(Market Price per share ÷ Earnings per Share)			
Dividend per Share	13.8	15.2	17.20
Dividend Yield	**3.92**	**4.31**	**4.88**
(Dividend per Share ÷ Market Price per Share x 100)			
Dividend Cover	**1.73**	**1.96**	**1.20**
(Earnings per Share ÷ Dividend per Share			

Shareholders' Funds (Ord. Shared + Res + Pref. Shares - if any)	387	378	378.8
Return on Equity	**0.05**	**0.03**	**0.04**
(Profit after Tax ÷ Shareholders' Funds)			
Share % for Young's by investing 10 million			**4.02**
((Amount invested/Share Price)/No. Of shares issued)*100			
Market capital			**248.65**
(No. Of shares issued x Share Price)			

APPENDIX – VI

Ratio Analysis for Nichol's plc

(The annual reports for the companies were obtained and are available in http://www.northcote.co.uk/)

Name of the company	Nichols plc (Vimto)		
Balance Sheet Analysis Spread Sheet	2004	2005	2006
Date of auditors certificate		22/3/2006	15/3/2007
(State if qualified)	n/q	n/q	n/q
Currency (in £)	£000's	£000's	£000's
QUICK ASSETS			
Cash & Bank	2988		7460
Short-term investments and deposits	2750		
Debtors/Accounts Receivable/Bills Receivable	13203	14592	12364
TOTAL QUICK ASSETS	**18941**	**14592**	**19824**
Stock - Finished Goods			
- Work in Progress	3987	3972	2169
- Raw Materials			
TOTAL CURRENT ASSETS	**22928**	**18564**	**21993**
CURRENT LIABILITIES			
Creditors/Accounts Payable/Bills Payable	4729	6415	4670
Hire Purchase/Leasing - less than one year			
Current Portion Long Term Debt	3499	5558	
(Secured Debt - memo item)			
Due to Group Companies			
Due to Directors			
Dividends			
Taxation - PAYE, NI, VAT etc.			
Corporation Tax	393	620	530
	1067	772	598

Accruals and deferred income	2293	4167	3166
Other Current Liabilities			
TOTAL CURRENT LIABILITIES	**11981**	**17532**	**8964**
LIQUID SURPLUS/(DEFICIT)	**10947**	**1032**	**13029**
QUICK ASSET SURPLUS/(DEFICIT)	**6960**	**-2940**	**10860**
FIXED AND OTHER ASSETS			
Freehold Properties	34	32	
Leasehold Properties	5942	5916	
Equipment, fittings & vehicles	7255	7615	3179
Investments - Subsidiaries			
Associates			
Others Unlisted investments			
Due from Group Companies			
Goodwill			
TOTAL FIXED AND OTHER ASSETS	**13231**	**13563**	**3179**
TEM AND OTHER LIABILITIES			
Future Taxation			
Deferred Taxation			
Hire Purchase/Leasing			
Loans Due for Repayment - one to five years	2592	750	
Loans Due for Repayment beyond five years			
Pension Liability	3723	4906	4553
Provision & charges	1393	1452	1184
	7708	**7108**	**5737**
Minority Interests			
TOTAL TERM & OTHER LIABILITIES	**7708**	**7108**	**5737**
NET TANGIBLE ASSSETS - SURPLUS/(DEFICIT)	**16470**	**7487**	**10471**
Financed by			

Shared Capital - Issued	3,697	3697	3697
Capital Reserves	3766	3766	3977
Distributable Reserves	10594	9528	11909
Less: (Goodwill and Intangibles)	-1587	-9504	-9112
SHAREHOLDERS FUNDS - SURPLUS/(DEFICIT)	**16470**	**7487**	**10471**
PROFIT SUMMARY			
Profit Before Interest and Tax	4820	6670	4775
Profit on sale of Fixed Assets	-11062		2166
Investment Income and Interest Receivable			
Profit Before Interest Paid	**-6242**	**6670**	**6941**
(Interest Paid)	-887	-707	58
Profit Before Tax(PBT)	**-7129**	**5963**	**6999**
(Taxation)	-1579	-1999	-1152
(Minority Interests)			
Extraordinary items			
Attributable Profit/Loss After Tax (APAT)	**-8708**	**3964**	**5847**
(Dividends)	-3253	-3309	-3407
Residual Profit/Loss	**-11961**	**655**	**2440**
Additional Capital and Reserve Movements		-1066	
Revaluation			
Exchange Losses		-1754	64
Goodwill W/O		-7917	392
NET VARIATION IN SURPLUS/ (DEFICIT)	**-11961**	**-10082**	**2896**
KEY FIGURES AND RATIOS			
Sales	88073	63336	52296
Cost of Goods Sold	51971	30235	24764

Gross Profit	36102	33101	27532
Depreciation	2061	2993	1306
Capital Employed	20649	17471	19583
PROFITABILITY			
Gross Profit Margin			
(Gross Profit ÷Sales x100)	41.0	52.3	52.6
Net Profit Margin			
(Residual profit ÷ Sales x 100)	-13.6	1.0	4.7
Return on Capital Employed			
(Profit Before Interest & Tax ÷	23.3	38.2	24.4
Capital Employed) x 100)			
CONTROL/LIQUIDITY			
Credit Given			
(Debtors ÷ Sales x 360)	54	83	85
Credit Taken			
(Creditors ÷ Cost of Goods Sold x 360)	33	76	68
Stock Turnover			
(Stock÷ Cost of Goods Sold x 360)	28	47	32
Current Ratio			
(Current Assets ÷ Current Liabilities) x 100	191.4	105.9	245.3
Liquid Ratio			
(Quick Assets ÷ Current Liabilities) x 100	158.1	83.2	221.2
GEARING AND SOLVENCY			
Gross Gearing			
(Total Borrowings ÷ Surplus)*100	36.98	84.25	0.00
Net Gearing			
(Net Borrowings ÷ Surplus)			
INVESTMENT RATIOS			
Profit after Tax	-8708	3964	5847

Preference Dividend (if any)	3253	3309	3475
Number of Ordinary Shares in Issue	36492387	36633627	36685868
Earnings per share in pence ('p')	**-23.86**	**10.82**	**15.94**
(Profit after Tax & Preference Dividend (if any) ÷			
Number of Ordinary Shares in Issue)			
Market Price per share as on (29-01-08)	222.5	222.5	222.5
Price / Earnings Ratio	**-9.32**	**20.56**	**13.96**
(Market Price per share ÷ Earnings per Share)			
Dividend per Share	8.8	8.95	9.40
Dividend Yield	**3.96**	**4.02**	**4.22**
(Dividend per Share ÷ Market Price per Share x 100)			
Dividend Cover	**-2.71**	**1.21**	**1.70**
(Earnings per Share ÷ Dividend per Share			
Share holders' Funds (Ord. Shared + Res + Pref. Shares - if any)	19636	16991	19583
Return on Equity	**-0.44**	**0.23**	**0.30**
(Profit after Tax ÷ Shareholders' Funds)			
Share % for Young's by investing 10 million			**12.25**
((Amount invested/Share Price)/No. Of shares issued)*100			
Market capital			
(No. Of shares issued x Share Price)			**81.63**

APPENDIX – VII

(The annual reports for the companies were obtained and are available in http://www.northcote.co.uk/)

Ratio Analysis for Thorntons plc

Name of the company	THORNTONS PLC		
Balance Sheet Analysis Spread Sheet	2005	2006	2007
Date of auditors certificate			
(State if qualified)	n/q	n/q	n/q
Currency (in £)	£000's	£000's	£000's
QUICK ASSETS			
Cash & Bank	874	932	2858
Short-term investments and deposits			
Debtors/Accounts Receivable/Bills Receivable	12775	11642	12628
TOTAL QUICK ASSETS	**13649**	**12574**	**15486**
Stock - Finished Goods	17787	11540	13772
- Work in Progress		2308	2409
- Raw Materials		1469	2021
TOTAL CURRENT ASSETS	**31436**	**27891**	**33688**
CURRENT LIABILITIES			
Creditors/Accounts Payable/Bills Payable	25548	5681	8028
Unsecured Bank Loans and Overdrafts	13933	930	19000
Finance Lease obligations		4152	3577
(Secured Debt - memo item)			
Due to Group Companies			
Due to Directors			
Dividends			
Taxation - PAYE, NI, VAT etc.	1616	832	1418
Other Taxation		3559	2409
Provision & charges	52	142	181

Accruals and deferred income		9645	9247
Other Liabilities		185	175
TOTAL CURRENT LIABILITIES	**41149**	**25126**	**44035**
LIQUID SURPLUS/(DEFICIT)	**-9713**	**2765**	**-10347**
QUICK ASSET SURPLUS/(DEFICIT)	**-27500**	**-1522**	**10860**
FIXED AND OTHER ASSETS			
Long Leasehold & free hold Properties	7460	30559	29759
Short lease hold properties		2652	2513
Equipment & vehicles	72084	30826	27997
Fittings		5355	6109
Investments - Subsidiaries			
Associates			
Others Unlisted investments			
Due from Group Companies			
Computer Software		6027	5950
TOTAL FIXED AND OTHER ASSETS	**79544**	**75419**	**72328**
TERM AND OTHER LIABILITIES			
Unsecured Bank Loans and Overdrafts	15332	16000	0
Finance Lease obligations		7421	6692
Future Taxation			
Deferred Taxation	1577	2284	2512
Hire Purchase/Leasing			
Pension Liability	18997	17941	15417
Other Non Current Liabilities	1785	2093	1996
Provision & charges	565	491	478
	38256	**46230**	**27095**
Minority Interests			
TOTAL TERM & OTHER LIABILITIES	**38256**	**46230**	**27095**
SHAREHOLDERS FUNDS - SURPLUS/(DEFICIT)	**31575**	**31954**	**34886**
Financed by			

Ordinary Shares	6669	6724	6811
Share Premium	12528	12890	13551
Retained Earnings	12,378	12340	14524
SHAREHOLDERS FUNDS - SURPLUS/(DEFICIT)	**31575**	**31954**	**34886**
PROFIT SUMMARY			
Profit Before Interest and Tax	12555	17304	14600
Profit on sale of Fixed Assets	452	844	400
Investment Income and Interest Receivable			
Profit Before Interest Paid	**13007**	**18148**	**15000**
(Interest Paid)	-2526	-2360	-1824
Profit Before Tax(PBT)	**10481**	**15788**	**13176**
(Taxation)	-2429	-2013	-1463
(Minority Interests)			
Extraordinary items			
Attributable Profit/Loss After Tax (APAT)	**8052**	**13775**	**11713**
(Dividends)	-4428	-4443	-4512
Residual Profit/Loss	**3624**	**9332**	**7201**
Additional Capital and Reserve Movements			
Revaluation			
Exchange Losses			
Goodwill W/O			
NET VARIATION IN SURPLUS/ (DEFICIT)	**3624**	**9332**	**7201**
KEY FIGURES AND RATIOS			
Sales	187704	176626	185989
Cost of Goods Sold	91276	84765	86022
Gross Profit	96428	91867	99967
Depreciation			

Capital Employed	31575	31954	34886
PROFITABILITY			
Gross Profit Margin			
(Gross Profit ÷ Sales x100)	**51.4**	**52.0**	**53.7**
Net Profit Margin			
(Residual profit ÷ Sales x 100)	**1.9**	**5.3**	**3.9**
Return on Capital Employed			
(Profit Before Interest & Tax ÷	**39.8**	**54.2**	**41.9**
Capital Employed) x 100)			
CONTROL/LIQUIDITY			
Credit Given			
(Debtors ÷ Sales x 360)	**25**	**24**	**24**
Credit Taken			
(Creditors ÷ Cost of Goods Sold x 360)	**101**	**24**	**34**
Stock Turnover			
(Stock ÷ Cost of Goods Sold x 360)	**70**	**65**	**76**
Current Ratio			
(Current Assets ÷ Current Liabilities) X 100	**76.4**	**111.0**	**76.5**
Liquid Ratio			
(Quick Assets ÷ Current Liabilities) x 100	**33.2**	**50.0**	**35.2**
GEARING AND SOLVENCY			
Gross Gearing			
(Total Borrowings ÷ Surplus)*100	**92.68**	**52.98**	**54.46**
Net Gearing			
(Net Borrowings ÷ Surplus)			
Gearing (Total Liabilities)			
OTHER KEY FIGURES			
Capital Expenditure			
Capital Commitments: Contracted			
Authorised			

Contingent Liabilities: Guarantees			
Other			
Leasing Obligations			
Director's Remuneration			
INVESTMENT RATIOS			
Profit after Tax	5550	3648	5296
Preference Dividend (if any)	3253	4443	4512
Number of Ordinary Shares in Issue	65118846	65440406	66346144
Earnings per share in pence ('p')	**8.52**	**5.57**	**7.98**
(Profit after Tax & Preference Dividend (if any) ÷			
Number of Ordinary Shares in Issue)			
Market Price per share as on (29-01-08)	140	140	140
Price / Earnings Ratio	**16.43**	**25.11**	**17.54**
(Market Price per share ÷ Earnings per Share)			
Dividend per Share	4.85	4.85	4.85
Dividend Yield	**3.46**	**3.46**	**3.46**
(Dividend per Share ÷ Market Price per Share x 100)			
Dividend Cover	**1.76**	**1.15**	**1.65**
(Earnings per Share ÷ Dividend per Share			
Shareholders' Funds (Ord. Shared + Res + Pref. Shares - if any)	31575	31954	34886
Return on Equity	**0.18**	**0.11**	**0.15**
(Profit after Tax ÷ Shareholders' Funds)			

Share % for Young's by investing 10 million			**10.77**
((Amount invested/Share Price)/No. Of shares issued)*100			
Market capital			**92.88**
(No. Of shares issued x Share Price)			

Pro Forma Balance Sheet of Young & Co for 2008					
(State if qualified)	n/q	Revaluation of Properties	Loans	Investment	Total
Currency (in GBP £000's)_____)					
QUICK ASSETS					
Cash & bank	999				999
Debtors/Accounts Receivable/Bills Receivable	71,536				71,536
TOTAL QUICK ASSETS	72,535				72,535
Finished goods	1,431				1,431
Work-in-progress					
Raw materials					
TOTAL CURRENT ASSETS	73,966				73,966
CURRENT LIABILITIES					0
Short term borrowings	58,184				58,184
Other creditors	23,383				23,383
TOTAL CURRENT LIABILITIES	81,567				81,567
LIQUID SURPLUS/ (DEFICIT)	-7,601				-7,601
QUICK ASSET SURPLUS/(DEFICIT)	-9,032				-9,032
FIXED AND OTHER ASSETS					0
Tangible Fixed Assets	232,286	200,000			432,286
Plant & Equipment & fixtures & fittings					0
Fixtures & Fittings					

Investments – Subsidiaries	0			50,000	50,000
Associate Company	22,458				22,458
	254,744				504,744
TERM AND OTHER LIABILITIES					0
Bank loans due 1-5 years	43,979		50,000		93,979
Bank loans due 5 years+					0
Hire purchase					
Retirement Benefit Obligation	-669				-669
Provisions & charges	4,295				4,295
TERM & OTHER LIABILITIES	47,605				97,605
Minority Interests					
TOTAL TERM & OTHER LIABILITES	47,605				97,605
NET TANGIBLE ASSETS - SURPLUS/ (DEFICIT)	**199,538**				**399,538**
Financed by					0
Share Capital - Issued	6,028				6,028
Share Premium Account					
Capital Reserves	80,853	200,000			280,853
Distributable Reserves	114,780				114,780
Less Investment in own shares	-2,123				-2,123
SHAREHOLDERS FUNDS - SURPLUS/ (DEFICIT)	**199,538**				**399,538**